I0794460

Praise For

LEARNING FOR WISDOM

"This is a rare and timely treatise. Rare because it takes an important but sometimes perplexing topic, and renders it both accessible and moving. In that sense, it turns an obligation into a privilege. But for *the* Christian learner it is also an invitation to faithfulness. To grow in wisdom because there is no responsible alternative. *Learning for Wisdom* is a gift."

—**Stan D. Gaede,** President Christian College Consortium

"*Learning for Wisdom* should be required reading not only for every student who attends Christian college or university, but also for their parents. Indeed, I would hope that faculty at those colleges and universities as well as pastors and high school teachers whose members and students go to Christian colleges and universities should read this book about Christian education and the good life. Taylor writes clearly and profoundly about the nature and strengths of a Christian education."

—**Tremper Longman III,** Robert H. Gundry Professor of Biblical Studies, Westmont College

"James Taylor clearly and cogently develops the cultivation of theoretical, practical, and productive wisdom in the quest for truth, goodness, and beauty. This multi-faceted approach to wisdom underscores the biblical dynamic of loving, learning, and living well and the formation of virtue in all arenas of life. This well-crafted book invites us to treasure the interior life in such a way that being animates doing."

—**Kenneth Boa,** author, speaker, and president of Reflections Ministries, Atlanta, GA

"James Taylor captures the essential goal of Christian general education to balance learning for doing and for becoming. He systematically develops the interaction of Athens and Jerusalem, exhorting faculty and students to both master academic disciplines and be mastered by the Holy Spirit. Faculty who want to reflect deeply on their integrative task should consider this as their guidebook."

—**V. James Mannoia, Jr.,** President Emeritus, Greenville College

"*Learning for Wisdom* should be required reading for every Christian parent, youth leader, admissions counselor, and high school student thinking about college. In just over two hundred pages, Taylor answers three important questions: "Why College at all"; "Why a Christian College?"; and "What's the point of General Education?" In doing so, he introduces the reader to the rich literature about learning from the Christian, classical, and global traditions; prepares students for the contemporary climate of debate about learning on university campuses; and deepens our desire for lives as large and adventurous as God's calling. The discussion of sources and questions for reflection at the end of each chapter invite the reader to further personal exploration as well as to useful group engagement with the themes of the book."

—**Shirley A. Mullen**, president and professor of History, Houghton College

LEARNING *for* WISDOM

Christian Education

& the Good Life

JAMES E. TAYLOR

Westmont College

Abilene Christian University Press

LEARNING FOR WISDOM
Christian Education and the Good Life

ACU
PRESS

ISBN 978-1-68426-010-2

Printed in the United States of America

Library of Congress Cataloging-in-Publication Data is on file at the Library of Congress, Washington, DC

Cover design by ThinkPen Design, LLC
Interior text design by Sandy Armstrong, Strong Design

For information contact:
Abilene Christian University Press
ACU Box 29138
Abilene, Texas 79699

1-877-816-4455
www.acupressbooks.com

17 18 19 20 21 22 23 / 7 6 5 4 3 2 1

CONTENTS

Section Three: Learning for Wisdom

INTRODUCTION

Parents tell their children to get a good education. Why? So they can end up getting a good job—or so it can be natural to assume. This way of thinking about learning makes us think of our schooling as vocational training. We can end up viewing our education in this way even if we go to a university or a liberal arts college instead of a technical or vocational school that trains people for a special profession or career. A person may get a broader education at a college or university, but many assume the whole point is still the same: to be prepared for a career. Learning for doing. Not learning for being.

What would a good job be, anyway? Would it be one with a really high salary? If so, then the best way to pick a college would be to figure out which one would put you in the best position to make a lot of money after you graduate. You should also factor in how much an education at that college will cost so you can subtract the total from your expected earnings. How would a Christian college fare on this analysis? Many good Christian colleges are pretty expensive nowadays. Are they worth it? In today's job market, your chances of getting a high-paying job are a lot better if you have a college degree. So if you're looking for a good salary, you'll have to pay for a college education. But do you have to pay for a *Christian college* education to get a good job? Clearly not. There are obviously many cheaper ways to earn a bachelor's degree. So how could it make sense to put out a lot of money to go to a good Christian school? It can make sense for at least two reasons.

For one thing, there's more to life than making money. After all, the only reason we want money is to use it to get other things we want. It doesn't take too much thought to figure out what these other things are. Most of us want not only to get a good job but also to get married and have kids. Families need a place to live, food on the table, clothes to wear, and a way to get around. These things cost money. We want to make money so we can have these things. And these are just the bare necessities. We also need to see the doctor and the dentist. We need insurance of various kinds. We have to pay taxes. We also want extra money to enjoy ourselves (through entertainment, travel, etc.) and to give to others (who either need or want our help). Money isn't really any good by itself. We like to have it because we want to have all these other things.

For another thing, money can't buy the most important things in life. Though we might sometimes think, with the song from the Broadway musical *Cabaret,* that "money makes the world go 'round," we're more likely to agree with the Burt Bacharach song that "what the world needs now is love, sweet love," and the Beatles' musical observation that "money can't buy me love." It's true that it's hard to be happy without at least the basic things listed above that money *can* buy. But we all know people who have all those things and more who are profoundly unhappy—often because of a lack of love in their lives. It's hard to deny that we all have a need to love and to be loved. Isn't that the main reason many of us want to marry and have kids? We need love because we are not just bodies; we also have souls, and a big part of what goes along with having a soul is that we have the capacity for love and the need for it too.

Learning for Wisdom

Love isn't the only need of the soul that money alone can't meet. That's because there's more to our souls than our hearts. People have hearts, but they also have heads and hands. Since we have heads, we need to learn. Since we have hands, we need to labor. To have a soul is to have a need to love, to learn, and to labor. Or to put it another way, because we are the way we are, we have a need for union, for understanding, and for usefulness. It's true that people can *live* without these things. But they can't live *well*. To live, you need to have your bodily needs met (food, drink, shelter, clothing, etc.). To live well, you need to love, to learn, and to labor.

These are elements of the good life for human beings. But what does all this have to do with Christ? From a Christian standpoint, there is one human need that stands out above all the rest. This is our need for God. In the prayer with which St. Augustine begins his *Confessions*, he acknowledges to God that "our hearts are restless until they find their rest in Thee" (book 1, paragraph 1). Complete and eternal happiness, joy, peace, and rest require a heart that loves God and, further, loves God above everything else. The human needs mentioned in the previous paragraph can be understood from this perspective. When God created humans, he gave us bodies and souls. God designed our physical natures with certain physical needs, and God created the world in which we live to include the material resources for the satisfaction of these needs. God also created us in God's image. This means that our souls have capacities that reflect, though imperfectly, some of God's capacities. Among these are our capacities to learn, to love, and to labor. That is, God has made humans with minds, hearts, and hands. Human happiness requires that we use these God-given gifts to satisfy our needs and the needs of others—all to the glory of God.

All of us properly functioning human beings have these God-given gifts of the soul. We can all think, love, do, and make. However, not everyone is using these gifts to meet his or her needs for learning, loving, and leaving a legacy. Some may be using them, but using them in the wrong way. The proper use of these gifts requires *wisdom.* Wisdom is knowledge that really matters. If living well is what matters most, then the highest form of wisdom involves knowing how to live well. If living well requires genuine understanding, proper loving, and worthwhile contributing, then wisdom will take the form of knowing how to understand, to love, and to contribute as we should. From a Christian standpoint, wisdom tells us that we should understand the world as God's creation and ourselves as created by God in God's image. Wisdom also provides us with the knowledge of how to love as we ought to love: that we should love God most, then humans, and then other things. Wisdom also says that our contribution ought to further the kingdom of God and give glory to God.

This is part of what wisdom tells us in general. Where can wisdom be found? Some wisdom is *received,* and some is *achieved*. According to the Christian faith, we receive some wisdom in the form of God's revelation in the Bible. The truths about God and our relationship to him summarized in the previous paragraph are among those that count as wisdom we receive from God in this way. Many of these truths have to be taken on faith: they're not things we could figure out on our own. But there are a number of questions about God, the world, and human life that the Bible doesn't answer. Wisdom about these things, if it's possible for us to acquire it, must be achieved by learning. For this kind of wisdom, we need to use our God-given minds and hearts. We need to use our hearts to *love* the truths we seek and our minds to *learn* truths about ourselves and about the world in which we live.

This is where a general Christian education comes in. A *general* Christian education—as opposed to a *specific* one—prepares Christian students for wise and loving Christian living rather than just for a special activity, skill, job, occupation, career, or vocation. And though a general Christian education is based on the Bible—on what we receive by faith in God's word—it also goes *beyond* the Bible to include the wisdom we can achieve by means of the minds and hearts God gave us. Though there are other paths to wisdom, general Christian learning is one important way we can achieve the wisdom we do not receive. It can also help us better understand and appreciate the wisdom we do receive. As a result, such an education can help us *be* the kind of people who *effectively respond to God's call.* It can assist us in our efforts to love God and others more wisely. If a general Christian education can contribute to our being the sort of people God created us to be and to our living the sort of life God calls us to live, then general Christian learning is worthwhile indeed. But many people have concerns about the very idea of a general Christian education. They wonder whether it can really deliver the great good of wisdom as we have suggested it can. Of course non-Christians raise this question. But many Christians do as well, as illustrated by the hypothetical examples in the next section.

Questions and Concerns

Sam shuffled through the stack of glossy brochures on the table in front of him. Now that his junior year in high school was almost over, he needed to start thinking about college. He knew he wanted to get into a good school, but the variety of institutions bewildered him. Should he go to a state university, a secular college, a Christian college or university, or a Bible college? Since he was a Christian, he was considering going to a Christian school of some kind. But didn't a lot of Christians go to non-Christian colleges and universities? Wouldn't a Christian college be too cut off from the rest of the world? Couldn't he serve the Lord better by witnessing to non-Christians? Besides, his parents said most of the Christian colleges were too expensive. They said he could get an equally good or better education at a state university.

Mary felt nervous as she waited her turn to speak to her small group of fellow first-year students. It was orientation week at her Christian college. Mary and her peers were taking turns trying to answer the question posed by Steve, their junior class group leader. "Why *did* I choose to come to a place like this for college?" Mary wondered to herself. When it was her turn to speak, Mary listed the reasons that had occurred to her. She said she wanted to get a good education from

Christian professors in a Christian environment. She added her hope that this would strengthen her faith and help her find a job with which she could serve the Lord.

Mary's orientation group leader, Steve, was having trouble being fully attentive to his group members' contributions. He was recalling his first week at the college. He remembered the strange mix of anxiety and eagerness he had experienced. It struck him that his thoughts and expectations had been similar to many of those being voiced in this orientation group. But things had changed. He had come to this college to follow Christ and strengthen his faith. However, some of his courses seemed to him to be taught just as they would be at a secular institution. Either they had nothing to do with God, or they were about non-Christian ideas. Most troubling of all, he thought, were some of his religious studies classes that made him question what he believed. Steve was beginning to wonder about the value of a general Christian education for Christians, but he didn't share his concerns with the new students.

Later that month, Matt, a sophomore, was attending a worship service at a local church. The pastor had just finished preaching a sermon on the first couple chapters of 1 Corinthians. The pastor had explained that Paul was telling the Corinthians that they should seek God's wisdom and power instead of human learning and wisdom. Matt began to wonder why he was attending a Christian college. It occurred to him that he should have listened better to those at his home church who had cautioned him against attending a college that exposes people to dangerous ideas.

Months later, Samantha found herself both nostalgic and anxious. Now that her senior year was almost over, she reflected on her years at the college and wondered about her future. She remembered how, as a first-year student, she had wanted more than anything to change the world for Christ. Her desire had been reinforced by numerous chapel messages and by her participation in various campus ministries. However, her zeal was now muted by her growing appreciation for human diversity. Samantha was pleased with the way her general Christian education had broadened her sympathies. But now she wondered how she would combine her desire to transform the world for Christ with her conviction that differences—both among Christians and between Christians and non-Christians—need to be appreciated.

At some point, most students who attend (or consider attending) a Christian college or university ask these sorts of questions about the nature, value, and even possibility of a general Christian education. And these questions often reveal a mix of enthusiasm and concern. In many cases, the persistence of such questions can have behavioral consequences. A prospective student decides not to attend a Christian college. A current student drops out. Continuing students fail to get the most out of their college experience. A graduating student is disillusioned or aimless. Students' concerns about a general Christian education can have serious outcomes.

Each of these concerned individuals could benefit from a better perspective on the nature and value of general Christian learning. This superior perspective can lead to enhanced motivation. People who understand well the substance and aims of a general Christian education are more likely to be enthusiastic about it. Students are more likely to engage in it, to get the most out of it, to use its benefits throughout their lives, to support it, and to encourage their children to participate in it.

The purpose of this book is to provide readers with a perspective about general Christian learning that will ease concerns and strengthen enthusiasms. Hopefully, increased appreciation of this kind of education will lead to more meaningful involvement among those who choose to participate in it. The best way to engender interest in a type of education is to highlight its *value*—to showcase its benefits. Many Christians today have lost sight of the benefits of general Christian learning. One effective means of renewing their appreciation of these benefits is to explain the *nature* of a general Christian education. It's hard to be satisfied that something is worthwhile unless you understand it in the first place.

This book characterizes a general Christian education as "learning for wisdom." The ancient Greeks thought of wisdom as a virtue, like courage and self-control. Aristotle called wisdom an *intellectual* virtue—an excellence of the mind. So general learning is aimed at the acquisition of the intellectual virtue (or mental excellence) of wisdom. Once general studies are seen in this light, it becomes clearer why it would be worthwhile to engage in them. Wisdom is a valuable thing. It is honored both in the biblical tradition and in all parts of the world throughout human history. Those who possess it can be better off than those who do not. Wisdom is an essential ingredient in living the good life. Living well requires *exercising* the intellectual virtue of wisdom. With this connection to the good life, the value of general learning should be clear: general learning can lead to wisdom, and wisdom is a key component of the good life for human beings.

Tensions, Challenges, and Resources

The above sketch of the nature and value of general learning leaves a lot of questions unanswered and a lot of problems unsolved. One set of problems takes the form of apparent tensions between the tradition of general learning and the Christian faith. Here are three:

1. A general education emphasizes critical inquiry, open-mindedness, and academic freedom; Christian living emphasizes confident faith, commitment, and submission to God.
2. General learners achieve human wisdom on the basis of natural reason; Christian disciples receive divine wisdom on the basis of supernatural faith.
3. A general education requires mastery of a set of academic disciplines; Christian devotion requires being mastered by the Holy Spirit through the practice of spiritual disciplines.

Our case for the possibility of a Christian approach to general learning will consist in an attempt to resolve these apparent conflicts by characterizing general learning and Christian discipleship as mutually harmonious enterprises.

Another set of challenges involves a serious threat to assumptions *shared* by the classical tradition of general learning and the Christian faith. Some forms of contemporary "postmodernism" pose this threat. These postmodern views challenge the very idea of there being real answers to important questions of the sort raised in a general education and answered in a Christian theology and the other academic disciplines. In particular, some kinds of postmodern perspectives deny the existence of real truth and thus the value of pursuing it. They also reject the legitimacy of human reason as a means by which to search for, acquire, and sustain knowledge of truths about the world. An important part of advocacy for Christian general learning involves criticizing these postmodern assumptions.

The case for the value and possibility of a general Christian education makes use of both biblical and classical, nonbiblical sources. There is clearly no need to justify the use of the Bible to a Christian audience. However, some might balk at appeals to Plato, Aristotle, Augustine, and Aquinas. What could these ancient thinkers have to say that could possibly concern twenty-first-century readers? First, thinkers such as Plato and Aristotle had quite a lot to do with shaping the tradition of general education. For this reason alone, there is much value in considering their ideas. But furthermore, many of their ideas are still important contenders in the intellectual marketplace. They had a lot to do with initiating and setting the agenda for much of the intellectual conversation that is still taking place today. Their voices are still important, and they deserve to be heard along with more recent contributors. St. Augustine and St. Thomas Aquinas are important for being the first major Christian thinkers to try to integrate Christian theology with classical Greek philosophy. These medieval Christian philosophers were engaged in the same sort of project undertaken in this book: the integration of general learning and the Christian faith. We will do well to consider their thoughts on the matter.

Integrating general learning and the Christian faith requires at least resolving the three tensions between them mentioned above. The integration of faith and learning also involves combining the wisdom we receive from God's Word with the wisdom we achieve through learning about the world God created in such a way as to construct a Christian worldview. A Christian worldview is a distinctively Christian way of representing things as they truly are (a goal many postmodernists claim cannot be met).

But Christian general learning goes deeper than students being merely *properly intellectually informed* about the way things are from a Christian perspective as important as such a correct theoretical grasp of reality is. Christian general learning also has to do with Christian learners being *properly morally formed* in accordance with the character of a holy and loving God. That is, a general Christian education aims at the formation of both minds and hearts. Or rather, since students' minds and hearts have already been shaped in a number of ways for both good and ill by the time they show up on a Christian college or university campus, the purpose of general Christian learning is to help students follow the apostle Paul's advice to the church at Rome: "Do not conform to the pattern of this world, but *be transformed by the renewing of your mind.* Then you will be able to test and approve what God's will is—his good, pleasing and perfect will" (Rom. 12:2 NIV—emphasis mine). Since students' minds (and indeed *all* human minds) have already been *formed* in many ways that *conform* to an antibiblical pattern, their minds need to be *transformed.* The word "mind" in this verse is a translation of a Greek word (*nous*) that encompasses both how we think and what we value—or what we *love.* The change of mind Paul desires for his readers involves both seeing things as God sees them (knowing what is true) and loving things as God loves them (knowing how to love what one recognizes as good). But people acquire these sorts of knowledge—and others—only by means of *learning.*

A Note on Sources

St. Augustine recorded his search for the good life, culminating in his conversion to Christ and fulfillment in God, in his spiritual autobiography, *Confessions* (available in various English translations and editions). Aristotle's discussion of the intellectual virtues, including wisdom, can be found in his *Nicomachean Ethics* (various translations and editions), book 6. For a Christian perspective on the origin and nature of postmodernism and its challenges to the Christian church, see Stanley Grenz, *A Primer on Postmodernism* (Grand Rapids: Eerdmans, 1996). For a Christian critique of radical postmodernism, see Douglas Groothuis, *Truth Decay: Defending Christianity against the Challenges of Postmodernism* (Downers Grove: InterVarsity Press, 2000). *The Liberal Arts Tradition: A Documentary History* (Lanham: University Press of America, 2010), edited by Bruce A. Kimball, contains articles about the contributions of Plato, Aristotle, Augustine, and Aquinas, among many others, to the liberal arts (general learning) tradition.

Questions for Reflection and Discussion

1. Do you agree that a general Christian education ought to be focused primarily on learning for wisdom? Why or why not?

2. Do you share any of the concerns about a general Christian education possessed by the individuals featured in the second section of this chapter? If not, why not, and if so, what are your concerns?

3. The third section of this chapter mentions tensions in and challenges to general Christian learning. What kinds of resources do you think could help in resolving these tensions and meeting these challenges?

SECTION ONE

LEARNING

CHAPTER ONE

LEARNING

If you want to live a good life, you must find wisdom. One time-tested and valuable means to this end is to travel the path of disciplined, general learning. In order to navigate this path successfully, it will help if you know more about what learning really is. Learning is *a natural process that results in a gain of knowledge.* We can understand learning better by thinking carefully about this definition.

Learning and the Varieties of Knowledge

Let's focus first on the goal and eventual outcome of all learning: *knowledge.* People seek to learn in order to acquire knowledge. There are different kinds of knowledge. For example, John knows that Athens is the capital of Greece, he knows an act of kindness when he sees one, and he knows how to play guitar. We can label the three kinds of knowledge represented in these examples "*propositional* knowledge," "*recognitional* knowledge," and "*procedural* knowledge."

One thing that distinguishes these three types of knowledge is their *object.* The object of propositional knowledge is a *proposition*—a truth claim expressible by a declarative sentence. In the example, the proposition, or truth claim, is that Athens is the capital of Greece.

The object of recognitional knowledge is an individual thing or a characteristic of an individual thing. In the example, what John knows (is able to recognize or distinguish) is an act of kindness (or perhaps a person performing an act of kindness). Sometimes recognitional knowledge is called "experiential" or "acquaintance" knowledge. These alternative labels are appropriate. We can know something in the sense of recognizing it only by being acquainted with it through an experience of it.

The object of procedural knowledge is a procedure, a particular way of acting or accomplishing something. This kind of knowledge is often called a skill, an ability, or "know-how." To say that John knows how to play guitar is to say that John has the ability to perform the procedure or set of procedures we call "playing guitar." In sum, learning can lead to different types of knowledge. Let's sharpen our definition of learning by adding that learning is a natural process that results in a gain of *some kind of knowledge or other.*

We acquire distinct types of knowledge by means of different kinds of learning. Let's consider examples of the kinds of learning that lead to the three types of knowledge discussed above. We have different ways of talking about the kind of learning that leads to propositional knowledge. We call it "learning the truth," "getting the facts," or "acquiring information." Philosophers have had a lot to say about propositional learning. We'll say more about it below.

As for recognitional knowledge and learning, we might say that a student has learned to recognize a certain type of bad reasoning or is learning to identify a particular literary genre or wants to learn to name all the bones in a human skeleton.

Skill learning comes in a number of different forms. A chemistry student learns how to mix a solution or perform an experiment. A student in a composition class learns how to discipline herself to write one short essay a week. Another student is learning how to make good contributions in classroom discussions.

A good education includes each of these types of learning. Indeed, they are really inseparable. For instance, a student writes an essay for a course in American history. In the process, she learns some facts about a certain historical period, she learns to distinguish ethical questions from historical questions, and she learns how to engage in historical investigation.

There are two types of propositional knowledge that play an important role in a general education. One of these kinds has already been illustrated above by means of the example of knowing that Athens is the capital of Greece. As mentioned in the previous paragraph, when we come to have propositional knowledge of that sort, we say that we have learned a fact. But there is another important variety of propositional knowledge that we have not yet discussed. This is the sort of knowledge we have when we *understand* something. Clearly, it is possible to know that something is true without knowing *why* it is true. For instance, we can know that someone is knocking on our door without knowing *why* that person is knocking on our door. In that case we have knowledge that a proposition is true without knowing what *makes* that proposition true; there is something in that circumstance we do not understand. But when we open the door and our visitor explains why she has come to see us, we acquire additional propositional knowledge that is of the second kind: we come to know that our visitor was knocking on our door because she wanted us to sign her petition. And once we come to know that this proposition is true, we have an *explanation* by means of which we now understand something we previously knew to be true without knowing why it was true. Let's call the first type of propositional knowledge "fact propositional knowledge" and this second type of propositional knowledge "explanation propositional knowledge." Each of these types of propositional knowledge involves different kinds of learning. We learn facts by observation (e.g., that snow is white) and rational reflection (e.g., that white is a color). But we learn to understand a fact by means of reasoning about it.

Our definition of learning also characterizes it as a process resulting in a *gain* of knowledge. You engage in a process of learning in order to end up with something you don't have when you start out: new facts, new understandings, new perceptual capacities, and/or new skills. Of course, there may have been a time in the past when you had possession of some of these, but you forgot or got rusty. In that case, you engage in a process of *re*learning. But the result is the same: you move from a state of not knowing to a state of knowing. Moreover, knowing is always a good thing in some sense. Though your knowing something may have some negative effects (it may make you unhappy to know that people die of starvation, you may be repulsed when you recognize an act of brutality, or you may exercise a skill to do something bad), it is always good *in itself*. It is good to know the truth about something, to be able to recognize the way things really are, to be skillful in some way. In addition, since knowing is always a good thing, at least in itself (and often for what it leads to), learning is a good thing *for its own sake* too, since it essentially consists in the acquisition of knowledge. Finally, if learning and knowledge are good things, then they are worth caring about. Learning is a worthwhile activity.

Though there are varieties of knowledge and thus different kinds of learning, the kind of learning most prominent in historical discussions of a general education is learning that leads to propositional knowledge. A general education results, in part, in the acquisition of propositional knowledge (and in intellectual skills aimed at getting propositional knowledge). What is propositional knowledge? Philosophers give conflicting detailed answers to this question, but most would agree on something like the following general definition: what it is for you to have *propositional knowledge* is for you to *believe a truth on the basis of a sufficiently good reason*. So propositional knowledge involves true belief. But true belief isn't enough, since you can believe something that turns out to be true but believe it on the basis of a bad reason or on the basis of no reason at all. In that case, you are *lucky* that your belief is true—it's just an *accident*. Your true belief can be knowledge only if your believing the truth is not a result of luck or accident but instead the result of your being in possession of an adequate reason for thinking the proposition you believe is true. Plato used a helpful metaphor to distinguish knowledge from mere true belief or opinion. He said, "Knowledge differs from correct opinion in being *tied down*" (*Meno* 98a—emphasis mine). This characterization of propositional knowledge has an important consequence for general learning: the learning that results in propositional knowledge has a lot to do with thinking about *why* we believe something or should believe it. Such learning concerns a careful examination of reasons for belief.

Learning and the Sources of Knowledge

Not all propositional knowledge is "tied down" in the same way. Some of our knowledge is based on other things we know. For instance, Katie knows that Aristotle and Plato were fellow citizens on the basis of her knowledge that Plato was an Athenian citizen in 366 BCE and her knowledge that Aristotle was an Athenian citizen in 366 BCE. Is all of our knowledge like this? That is, is everything we know based on something else we know? Aristotle argued that the answer to this question is "no." His argument for this conclusion has become known as the "regress argument." The regress argument concludes that not all of our knowledge is based on other things we know. If this conclusion is true, then what makes some of our true beliefs instances of knowledge is that they are tied down to something other than knowledge (such as direct experience or insight). The way Aristotle put it is that not everything we know can be *demonstrated* to be true on the basis of other things we know. For suppose that all of our knowledge were demonstrable. If that were the case, then one thing Katie knows would be based on other things Katie knows, and those things would be based on still other things Katie knows, and on and on without ever stopping. This series of demonstrations is called a "regress." If all knowledge were demonstrable, then this regress would never stop—it would be infinite. An infinite regress could take the form of either an infinitely long *line* (a linear regress) or a *circle*, which by its very nature never stops (a circular regress). Either way, it is hard to see how the original bit of knowledge could be well-grounded—infinitely regressing demonstration chains don't seem to be capable of tying down knowledge. Aristotle concluded that some of our knowledge must be incapable of being demonstrated. Recently, some philosophers have taken issue with Aristotle's argument. However, whether one agrees with him or not, it seems clear that at least some of the things we know are based on other things we know. That is, our knowledge can grow. It can be extended. This feature of knowledge is important for those engaged in general learning to remember. What you know can be both the conclusion of one chain of reasoning and also the starting point in another chain of reasoning leading to further knowledge. Propositional knowledge has both roots and shoots.

Learning is also a *process*. We tend to think of learning as a *mental* process. That is, we are inclined to assume that learning is always a *conscious and deliberate cognitive activity*. But though much learning does involve our minds in this way, it is clear that there is also a significant amount of learning that does not. Young children learn how to crawl, walk, and talk without thinking about what they are doing. So at least some important kinds of procedural knowledge are acquired without the learner engaging in any significant degree of reflection. And this sort of learning doesn't stop when we grow up. We can learn how to get around our neighborhood just by taking regular walks in it. We can learn to recognize the tune of a song merely by repeated exposure to it. And we can learn to like people simply by being around them. Of course, we can also learn all these things by *trying* to learn them, but the present point is simply that such a conscious and deliberate effort is not required for learning. This distinction between conscious and sub- or unconscious learning will end up being very important for students at Christian colleges and universities—as we will see in Chapter Nine.

We may be tempted to say that all *conscious* learning is a mental process. However, it would be better to say that all conscious learning is *at least* a mental process. Obviously, conscious learning must involve the mind in some way, but it also often involves the body. For example, you can't learn to play guitar without using your hands, and you can't learn to recognize the color chartreuse without using your eyes. Clearly, all conscious learning intended to result in a gain of recognitional knowledge that requires the senses or an addition of procedural knowledge that involves the body will be a process that is both mental and physical.

Though different kinds of conscious learning involve different kinds of specific mental processes, all kinds of conscious learning involve such general mental processes as perceiving, attending, and remembering. Many philosophers and psychologists have agreed that conscious learning is a mental process with these general features. However, they have disagreed about the answers to the following two questions: (1) What mental process is *primary* in acquiring propositional knowledge? and (2) What makes a process *mental*? The philosophers Plato and Aristotle debated the first question in ancient times, and it continues to be a subject of controversy. Those who side with Plato can be called "innatists." People who prefer Aristotle's position are labeled "empiricists." The second question is the focus of a contemporary debate between "behaviorists" and "cognitivists." What follows is a brief account of each of these two debates.

What is the role of the mind in acquiring propositional knowledge? Plato argued that we come to know something by *remembering* it after having forgotten it. In that case, we don't really *learn* anything as much as *re*learn it. How could this be? Plato illustrated his view with an example involving two apparently equal lines (*Phaedo* 74–76). When we see the lines, we judge them to be equal. But we are also aware that no two lines in the physical world are *perfectly* equal. Plato asked how we could come to think of the lines as equal unless we already had the idea of (perfect) equality before we saw the lines. If we don't get our idea of equality from *perceiving* things, then where do we get it? Plato argued that this idea is *innate*; that is, we are born with it. He also said we aren't aware of our innate ideas until we perceive something that reminds us of them. For instance, we don't think about equality until we see apparently equal things. When we see apparently equal things, we are reminded of the idea of equality. This example helps explain why Plato thought that what the mind does in "learning" is really remembering.

Aristotle and his advocates denied Plato's claim that we have innate ideas. Aristotle initiated the idea that our minds are "blank slates" at birth. He believed that all our knowledge originates in our experience of the world by means of our five senses. Our sensory experience provides us with the foundational knowledge that is not demonstrated on the basis of other things we know but instead serves as a basis for furthering our knowledge. So Aristotle believed that the role of the mind in learning is to transform what we perceive with our senses into something we can know with our minds. Our minds also enable us to take this experientially derived knowledge and extend our knowledge on the basis of it.

This debate between Plato and Aristotle has been repeated throughout history. As said above, their views have come to be labeled *innatism* and *empiricism*, respectively. The Christian thinker St. Augustine held a view similar to Plato's in that he affirmed the possibility of nonsensory knowledge. Later, St. Thomas Aquinas formulated a version of Aristotle's view. Both these Christian philosophers had the advantage of appealing to God in explaining how humans acquire knowledge. St. Augustine held that God illumines our minds to grasp truths that are not accessible to our senses. Aquinas argued that God illumines our minds to enable us to turn our sensory experience of the world into knowledge about it.

This innatist–empiricist debate has important implications for general learning. If Plato and St. Augustine are right, then there is an important sense in which learners already have within themselves the seeds of their learning and eventual knowing. Plato believed that people learn best by conversing with a teacher who knows how to ask good questions and to use illustrations that trigger the learner's recollection of the truth. He thought his own teacher, Socrates, was an excellent example of this educational method. Many educators have adopted the Socratic method of critical questioning as their primary mode of instruction. On the other hand, if Aristotle and St. Thomas Aquinas are correct in holding that the mind is like a blank slate at birth and that learning must be based on sensory experience, then the teacher's job will be different in some respects. Initially, good instruction would involve guiding students in their observations of the world. Ultimately, the role of the teacher would be to help students reason about what they have observed. An example will help illustrate the difference between these two educational approaches. The eleventh-century Platonist philosopher St. Anselm believed that he could prove that God exists just by means of rational reflection on an innate concept of God. Later, the Aristotelian philosopher Aquinas denied that this was possible but argued that God's existence could be proven on the basis of observations of certain features of the world. This debate continues today among many Christian students and teachers. A good general Christian education will make room for both points of view.

More on Learning as a Process

Let's continue thinking about the definition of learning as a process that results in a gain of knowledge. According to behaviorists such as B. F. Skinner, the process of learning can be completely characterized in terms of the modification of human behavior on the basis of environmental stimuli and reinforcement. On this view, knowledge of various kinds is characterized in terms of actual behavior or dispositions to behave in certain ways in certain kinds of environments. The "mental" process of learning and the "mental" state of knowledge are defined on this view in terms of how the learner/knower acts or has a tendency to act. For instance, one learns to recite a poem from memory by means of repeated sensory exposures to the poem and rewards for correct recitation (such as the approval of a teacher). Once one's behavior has been modified in this way, one can be said to know that poem. But what it is to know the poem is simply to be able to recite it without external helps.

Cognitivists object that at least some human learning involves not only environmental stimuli and behavioral response but also intermediate internal cognitive processing (thinking). For instance, people learn not only how to recite a poem but also what the poem *means*. This latter kind of learning, according to cognitivists, requires people to reflect on the poem in light of their background knowledge about various things. Consequently, the process of learning and the state of knowing the meaning of a poem cannot be characterized in purely behavioral terms according to cognitivists. Today, most psychologists are cognitivists about learning; that is, they think that much learning involves mental processes that cannot be characterized solely in terms of how learners act or might act in certain circumstances. They think you can explain many learning processes only in terms of the inner, private, conscious mental—or "cognitive"—states of the learner.

Behaviorists tend to classify all knowing as *procedural* knowing. Since learning, for a behaviorist, involves acquiring a disposition or habit to behave or act in certain ways in certain circumstances, the outcome of learning can always be described in terms of knowing how to do something. Consequently, if behaviorism were a true theory, then all learning would be training in skills. On the other hand, if the cognitivists are right, then not all knowledge is procedural and not all learning is training. Cognitivism allows for a broader variety of kinds of learning and knowing.

There are some very important kinds of learning that aren't easily explained by either behaviorism or cognitivism. Recall the distinction between conscious and unconscious learning and the examples employed to illustrate the latter (learning how to get around your neighborhood, learning to recognize a tune, learning to like someone). Unconscious learning isn't something we *do*; it's something that *just happens to us*. And because it isn't deliberate, it's *automatic*. Moreover, though some unconscious learning results only in a disposition to *behave* in a certain way (such as when we unthinkingly slow down when the driver in front of us does), other instances of unconscious learning produce changes in our noncognitive *attitudes*. Learning to like someone is a case in point. Our attitude toward a person can change simply as a result of spending time with him or her. Associating regularly with some people can make us want to be with them more often. Importantly, unconscious learning can affect our desires, preferences, and values.

Why is unconscious learning important? Because as St. Augustine said, what is most important about us is what and how we love. And what we have learned to desire, prefer, and value—whether consciously or unconsciously—is what we have learned to love. According to Jesus, God wants us to learn to love God with everything we've got and to love other human beings as we love ourselves (Matt. 22:36–40, Mark 12:28–34, and Luke 10:25–28). The problem is that we aren't very good at doing either one of these things. And one of the biggest reasons for our failure to love both God and others as we should is that we live in a fallen world that has shaped our hearts to love the wrong things (or the right things in the wrong ways). Much of this shaping of our hearts—this formation of our desires—has been relatively unconscious and automatic. It has resulted simply from our living in a world characterized by rebellion against God. As we will see, in order to learn to love as we should, we need to put ourselves deliberately into contexts in which God can change our hearts—contexts in which we can cooperate with God by engaging in practices that will help us learn to have godly desires.

Ideally, a Christian college or university will provide the kind of community in which Christian students can experience learning how to love rightly. But in order for such learning to take place, it will not be enough for students' minds to be *informed* by means of their coming to have more propositional knowledge (as important as that kind of knowledge is). Their hearts will also need to be *formed* by means of their practice of spiritual disciplines. That is, though Christian students will need the kind of knowledge that can be *taught*, they will also need the kind of knowledge that can only be *caught*.

Finally, our definition of learning classifies it as a *natural* mental process. This qualification is meant to convey the idea that human beings are learners *by nature*. Whether we humans are born with some form of knowledge (as the innatists say) or our minds are instead like blank slates waiting to be written on (as the empiricists say), all agree that we are born with the capacity to learn. Moreover, as we've seen, much of our learning takes place naturally and automatically without the aid of human teachers and artificial (human-made) instructional tools and resources. Indeed, one thing that impresses the linguist Noam Chomsky is the extent to which young children are able to learn a natural human language with relatively little deliberate instruction on the part of adults. Children learn a lot even when they are not instructed. This is not to say, of course, that it is not possible or worthwhile for students to engage in a more formal and deliberate education involving teachers and a carefully designed curriculum. Teaching is an art that involves human cooperation with nature to facilitate the student's acquisition of knowledge. So to say that learning is a natural process is not to say that it cannot or should not benefit from the human art of teaching as an aid to nature—an art that is central to a general education.

A Note on Sources

Plato's characterization of knowledge (vs. correct opinion) as "tied down" occurs in his dialogue *Meno*. In both this dialogue and his dialogue *Phaedo*, Plato portrays Socrates as arguing for the view that knowledge is innate. Aristotle's regress argument is located in his *Posterior Analytics*, book 1, chapter 3, and his claim that human minds are "blank slates" at birth can be found in his *De Anima* (*On the Soul*), 429b29–430a1. St. Augustine's *De Magistro* (*On the Teacher*) contains his account of nonsensory knowledge via divine illumination, and many passages in his *Confessions* illustrate this account. St. Thomas Aquinas's more empiricist theory of the role of divine illumination in knowledge can be found in his *Summa Theologica* (his comprehensive treatise of Christian theology), 1a, 75–89, where he distinguishes Augustine's view from his own more Aristotelian view. See St. Anselm's *Proslogion* for his attempt to prove God's existence on the basis of the concept of God (Anselm's "ontological" argument for God's existence), and see Aquinas's denial that this is possible and alternative experience-based arguments for God's existence in his *Summa Theologica*, part 1, question 2. B. F. Skinner articulates his behaviorist theory of learning in *Science and Human Behavior* (New York: Free Press, 1953), Noam Chomsky formulates his cognitivist (and innativist) account of language learning in *Rules and Representations* (New York: Columbia University Press, 1980), and Chomsky critiques Skinner's theory in his review of Skinner's *Verbal Behavior* (in the journal *Language* 35, no. 1 [1959]: 26–58). St. Augustine's affirmation that what is most important about us is what and how we love is located in *De Civitate Dei* (*The City of God*), book 15, chapter 22.

Questions for Reflection and Discussion

1. Which type of knowledge discussed in the first section of this chapter do you think is most important, if any, and why do you think so?

2. Are you an "innatist" or an "empiricist" about the origin of knowledge? And do you learn best by responding to questions or reflecting on what you observe?

3. Do you agree that unconscious learning is important? Why or why not?

CHAPTER TWO

GENERAL LEARNING

MUCH HUMAN LEARNING IS FOR SPECIFIC PURPOSES, BUT OUR FOCUS in this book is on *general* human learning. The aim of general human learning is comprehensive human development. It concerns the actualization of human potential for excellence in a wide range of categories. The focus of general education is primarily on *being* a certain general kind of person and only secondarily on *doing* certain particular kinds of things. The goal of general education is to cultivate wise, good, and skillful people—no matter what their specific personal, social, and vocational involvements are. Historically, at least in "Western" societies, general education is rooted in the "liberal arts" educational tradition.

Two Competing Ideals

According to Bruce A. Kimball, the history of liberal arts education is a history of two competing ideals. The "philosophical ideal" can be traced back to the ancient Greek philosopher Socrates. The "oratorical ideal" is rooted in the Roman statesman Cicero. This chapter's characterization of the oratorical and philosophical traditions is somewhat loosely based on Kimball's discussion. The following remarks about these two traditions will serve conceptual purposes more than historical ones. The philosophical model and the oratorical model pull in different directions. However, they also share some common ground. In sketching these two approaches to the liberal arts, we will be more concerned with providing possibilities for thinking about the nature of general learning than with reporting historical facts. As a result, we will portray the two types rather starkly as contrasting paradigms in a way that may not be completely faithful to their actual origins. Once we have a general grasp of these two traditions, we will consider a conception of general learning that both maintains the tension between them and provides a home for the Christian faith. We will characterize this inclusive model in terms of the nature, purpose, methods, and content of a general education.

Though rooted in Athens, liberal education flowered later in Rome as an outworking of the oratorical ideal. Under the tutelage of Cicero, liberal education was aimed at training citizens to be leaders of society. What made the education *liberal* is that it was an education for free citizens with the leisure to study ("liberal" comes from the Latin *liberales*, meaning "suitable for a free man"—a *liber*). What this meant at the time is that the students of the liberal arts were *wealthy free men*. The poor had to work and so did not have the leisure to study. Slaves were neither citizens nor free for study. Women were not citizens either. Since the purpose of liberal education was to train free men to lead society, it was primarily *practical*. A good leader is someone who is able to practice good leadership. What makes one capable of practicing good leadership is the possession of wisdom, moral virtue, and eloquence. Thus, in the oratorical tradition, a good liberal education would involve instruction that would lead to the possession of these personal attributes. Classical texts were used as the basis for the cultivation of these traits. Oratorical educators assumed these classical works to contain statements of important truths, models of genuine virtues, and examples of eloquent speeches. In this tradition, the knowledge acquired by liberal learning was valuable primarily as an instrument enabling its possessors to be good leaders in the community. Moreover, the true test of the possession of genuine wisdom was a person's ability to communicate it eloquently.

The philosophical ideal for liberal education is embodied in the Greek philosopher Socrates. This approach can be best understood by thinking about Socrates's famous claim that "the unexamined life is not worth living" (Plato, *The Apology* 37e–38a). What Socrates meant by this statement is that in order for our lives to be worthwhile, we must carefully examine our opinions and values to see whether or not they are really true and good. After critically scrutinizing his own important beliefs and values, Socrates claimed to be ignorant about what is ultimately true and best. Moreover, he cross-examined a number of his contemporaries who claimed to be wise and good. In doing so, he used what has become known as the "Socratic method" of critical questioning to show that these so-called authorities were not nearly as wise as they thought they were. Socrates applied his disposition to question authority to books as well. As far as he was concerned, books are not repositories of truth to be digested but instead records of thinking to be critically engaged. When all was said and done, Socrates persisted in being skeptical about the possibility of knowing the answers to the important questions he raised. Nonetheless, he believed that if he stopped pursuing the truth about these things, his life would no longer be worth living.

This emphasis on the perpetual *pursuit* of truth distinguishes the philosophical ideal of liberal education from the oratorical model. Socrates contrasted himself with the "sophists," who claimed to be wise (the Greek word is *sophos*). Instead, he called himself a *lover* of wisdom (in Greek, *philo* + *sophos*). You can love wisdom without being in possession of it. If you love it but don't have it, you will want to pursue it and try to acquire it. If you are sufficiently skeptical, your pursuit of truth may become perpetual. Though Socrates was primarily interested in pursuing the truth about matters of morality, later philosophers extended the Socratic quest to include speculation about ultimate reality.

Plato and Aristotle believed that pursuing the truth about such speculative matters was the best way for a human being to spend time. Thus the philosophical approach to liberal learning came to be characterized by a perpetual search for the answers to questions about theoretical and speculative matters. They considered knowledge about these things, if one could ever attain it, to be not only the best kind of knowledge but also worth having for its own sake whether it had any practical value or not. For these philosophers, though moral virtues like courage and self-control were considered important for the sake of good citizenship, intellectual virtues like knowledge and theoretical wisdom were even more important and were necessary for good scholarship.

The primary differences between the oratorical ideal of a liberal arts education and the philosophical model, as characterized above, are summarized in the following table. The contrasting phrases should be thought of as differences in *emphasis*:

The Oratorical Ideal of Liberal Learning	The Philosophical Ideal of Liberal Learning
Emphasis on the practical goal of good living	Emphasis on the theoretical goal of true believing
Acquisition of moral virtues is best	Acquisition of intellectual virtues is best
Relatively dogmatic	Relatively skeptical
Primarily oriented to community life	Primarily oriented to individual study
Education for good citizenship	Education for good scholarship
Accent on pursuit of goodness	Accent on pursuit of truth
More value placed on effective speaking	More value placed on logical thinking
Knowledge valued as an instrument	Knowledge valued for its own sake
Pragmatic political orientation	Speculative metaphysical orientation
Emphasis on the possession of wisdom	Emphasis on the pursuit of wisdom

These two competing liberal arts ideals continue to be a topic of conversation and debate today—even among students at Christian liberal arts colleges and universities (though they may use different language to express these two views). Whenever you witness or participate in a discussion in the dining commons or residence halls about whether a Christian general education should prepare students mostly for a life of Christian service or instead primarily for a habit of lifelong learning, you are observing an interchange of the sort initiated by the orators and philosophers. You may sometimes even find yourself wrestling with this question in your own mind. And you might find yourself attracted to each of these diverse approaches to general learning at different times—or even at the same time.

Common Ground

Fortunately, in spite of their differences, these two ideals also share some significant common ground. In particular, they are both agreed in their rejection of (1) educational sophism and (2) educational utilitarianism.

Let's look at educational sophism first. The sophists were described above as counterparts to Socrates who thought they were wise. Sophists were itinerant teachers in ancient Greece who offered instruction in things that fostered success. In particular, they taught people the information and skills they would need to be effective public speakers. The art of persuasion could be especially valuable in a democratic society such as Athens. The orators and philosophers were not so much averse to education in the discipline of rhetoric (indeed, rhetoric has pride of place among the orators) as much as they were against the sophist's abuses of argumentation. The sophistic tendency to pervert the art of rhetoric is immortalized in their boast to be able to teach their students "how to make the weaker argument into the stronger." The problem with this approach, of course, is that it makes arguments into instruments of manipulation rather than tools for seeking truth. Both the orators and the philosophers oppose this abuse of logic and rhetoric because both groups value truth over merely making something *pass* for true in order to come out ahead.

Educational utilitarianism is the view that an education is worthwhile only if it provides training in a specialized profession or vocation. From the standpoint of the educational utilitarian, both an oratorical and a philosophical liberal arts education are too general to be of much use. What is needed instead, these educational utilitarians think, is instruction in the technical methods of a particular occupation. The kind of knowledge favored on their view is what we called "procedural knowledge" in the previous chapter. Orators and philosophers are united in their condemnation of the utilitarian approach to education as overly narrow and restricted. Though the former two groups agree that an education can and should be useful in some sense, they also think that the best education will involve the "cultivation of humanity," to use the ancient Roman philosopher Seneca's phrase. A liberal arts education—as opposed to special vocational, professional, or technical training—is *general* enough to enhance the life of any normal adult human being regardless of his or her particular career. Another way to put this same point is that a liberal education is a *humanistic* education. It is an education intended to develop general human capacities.

This characterization of general learning as opposed to vocational training does diverge in one important respect from the views of some philosophers and orators. In saying that a general education is meant to profit *any normal adult human being*, we have introduced a democratic element that is not present in every version of the philosophical and oratorical ideals. Early versions of both of these models were clearly *aristocratic* in their orientation. As said above, the word "liberal" (*liberalis* in Latin) in "liberal arts" was originally meant to restrict such an education to people with adequate freedom and leisure to benefit from such an education. Given the political realities of ancient Greece and Rome, this meant that a liberal education was for wealthy male citizens. This restriction, however, seems more due to the accidents of the political situation than to the essence of a general education. A more democratic society, such as our own, provides a setting in which more people have the resources to enjoy and benefit from a general education.

In sum, though the orators and philosophers disagree in some important ways about the nature and purpose of a liberal education, they agree about two very important things: (1) a liberal education *values truth and reason,* and (2) a liberal education *is both general and humane.* These two common convictions provide a basis for a conception of general learning that can accommodate both the oratorical and philosophical traditions. It can also be integrated with the Christian faith, as we will see in the next chapter. Let us turn now to consider this inclusive approach to general learning.

An Inclusive Framework for General Learning

Any good framework for general education will give an account of the nature, purpose, methods, and content of such an education. The following framework makes use of the agreements of the orators and philosophers.

Consider first the *nature* of general learning. Essentially, a general education is a *humane* education. That is, it is a course of study that emphasizes the cultivation and perfection of certain human abilities and capacities. In Aristotle's terms, a general education is an education that *actualizes* a certain range of human *potential.* What range of human potential is this? That is, what is the *scope* of general learning? Normal human beings are born with a variety of physical and psychological capacities. These capacities combine to constitute an individual human being's potential for growth, development, maturation, and education. These inborn potentialities are actualized in human beings as a result of their interactions with their environments over time. Some of these changes are relatively automatic, and some require more conscious deliberation. Moreover, some of the changes have more to do with the body, and some are more involved with the mind. As we saw in the previous chapter, learning is a natural process that results in a gain of knowledge. So learning (even when it is unconscious) involves changes to a person's mind. Since learning is a *natural* process, it can occur without deliberate effort on the part of the learner. It can occur rather passively, without the intervention of a teacher. However, *general* learning requires a deliberate, disciplined engagement of the learner in a program of study that is designed to cultivate human intellectual capacities. Let's adopt Aristotle's terminology and call these cultivated human mental capacities "intellectual virtues." In sum, then, the nature and scope of a general education is the deliberate cultivation and refinement of human intellectual virtues.

What is the *purpose* of a general education? That is, what are the desired results of the cultivation of human intellectual virtues? Intellectual virtues are the abilities to use one's mind well. So a general way to state the purpose of a general education is to say that it is an education that enables you to use your mind well. Can we be more specific? You can use your mind well in a variety of ways and for a variety of purposes. Following Aristotle, we can identify three general and important purposes for which we can use our minds well. We can use our minds (1) to think about what's true, (2) to live a good life, and (3) to make and enjoy beautiful and useful things. Our intellectual virtues contribute to our capacity for reflection, action, and creation.

As said above, the orators and philosophers agreed about the value of *truth*. That is, both groups assumed that the truth is something that is worth pursuing and also possessing if possible. Many human intellectual virtues can be characterized in terms of the search for or the possession of truth. These include calculating, estimating, hypothesizing, reasoning, questioning, knowing, and remembering. But the orators and philosophers also valued *goodness* and *beauty*. Intellectual virtues that are cultivated for the sake of living a good life include imagining, deliberating, discerning, valuing, planning, deciding, and evaluating. Among those virtues with beauty in view are perceiving, imagining, inventing, organizing, measuring, evaluating, and designing. So we might say that the purpose of a general education is to inculcate all the general intellectual virtues that have truth, goodness, and beauty as objectives.

This is on the right track, but it needs to be qualified. As mentioned in the previous chapter, a kind of learning traditionally considered most prominent in a general education is learning that leads to propositional knowledge. Also, we characterized propositional knowledge as knowledge of the *truth* about something. On this view, the intellectual virtues aimed at truth are central in general learning. But this model also accommodates the goals of goodness and beauty. Among the truths to be known, if possible, are truths about how to live a good life and truths about how to make and enjoy beautiful and useful things. We will discuss knowledge of these sorts of truths in Section Two (in which the topic is wisdom) and the sorts of learning that result in knowledge of these truths in Section Three (where our focus will be on learning for wisdom).

A general education concerns the acquisition of human intellectual virtues primarily for the pursuit and possible possession of truth. What *methods* will enable general learners and their teachers to attain this end? Since a primary goal of general learning is propositional knowledge of various sorts, and since human beings grasp propositions by means of *language*, the methods of general learning will involve various uses of language. Chief among these uses of language are reading, writing, speaking, and listening. These methods will be employed in general learning both in order to *understand* and in order to *know*. You can't know something to be true unless you first understand what it means. If you're reading or listening, you won't be able to understand what someone claims to be true unless he or she expresses it clearly. Even if you understand a claim someone has said or written, you may not agree with the person unless he or she argues logically and convincingly for it. Whether you are the one communicating and arguing or the one listening and evaluating, you will need to be skilled in language use, reasoning, and convincing.

This brings us to the subject of the *content* of general learning. The original three subjects covered in a liberal arts education were grammar, logic, and rhetoric. These subjects cover the skills just mentioned: language use, logical reasoning, and effective communication. These areas of study really are at the heart of a general education. Later, the four subjects of arithmetic, geometry, music, and astronomy were added. These seven subjects constituted the *septem artes liberales.* Whereas the first three liberal arts are verbal, the latter four are mathematical. So a complete general arts education requires the use of methods that depend on both linguistic and mathematical skills (though there is a sense in which the linguistic skills are more fundamental, since mathematics is taught by means of language, but language-based subjects are not taught by means of mathematics). The exercise of mathematical skills enables students to think and communicate about relatively abstract and formal features of reality in nonlinguistic ways. These nonverbal means of conceptualizing and representing the world include the ways of thinking about measurable quantities used by scientists who seek knowledge about the quantifiable aspects of nature and society.

Today, the typical general education curriculum includes the *humanities* (philosophy, history, literature, and the creative arts), the *natural sciences* (physics, chemistry, biology, and part of psychology), the *social sciences* (social psychology, sociology, anthropology, political science, and economics), and the *formal sciences* (mathematics, logic, and computer science). This may seem like a "grab bag" without a unifying theme. However, all these disciplines combine to provide the learner with the *general* intellectual skills and knowledge needed to understand oneself, others, and the world in which we live together.

Most of the academic disciplines listed in the previous paragraph can be classified as "theoretical" academic disciplines. Theoretical academic disciplines are academic disciplines involving people who are devoted to the pursuit of propositional knowledge about the subject matter of those disciplines and who employ the methods characteristic of those disciplines. We'll use the word "science" (which is based on the Latin word *scientia*, which means "knowledge") to denote this kind of discipline. Our use of this word here is broader than its typical employment, which encompasses only the search for truth on the basis of *empirical* methods. Empirical methods for acquiring knowledge are methods that depend on the use of our five senses to observe the world around us and/or the use of our introspection to become acquainted with what is going on in our own minds. So for our purposes, mathematics and logic count as sciences, since they involve the quest for knowledge of certain kinds of truths—even though the methods employed in these disciplines are nonempirical.

An empirical science is a means of acquiring knowledge that requires empirical methods. More specifically, an empirical science requires justification of the truth claims of that science on the basis of experience. In contrast, a nonempirical science is a means of acquiring knowledge that does *not* require experience to justify its truth claims. When we list both empirical and nonempirical sciences, we will have at least the empirical *natural* sciences (that aim at knowledge of the natural world and the things in it created by God), the empirical *social* sciences (that seek knowledge about aspects of the world that are a product of human consciousness and social interaction), and the nonempirical or "a priori" *formal* sciences of logic, mathematics, and part of computer science. As we will see in the next chapter, there are two important sciences that are not included in this list but figure centrally in a *Christian* general education. These are the sciences of theology (the study of God) and of philosophy (insofar as it is possible for us to have philosophical *knowledge*). Moreover, as we will see in Chapter Eleven, we will need to add the creative arts to these sciences in order to have a complete general education curriculum (as we saw in the previous chapter, learning involves both "knowing that" and "knowing how").

Though the intellectual virtues involved in the *sciences* are focused on the acquisition of *propositional* knowledge, it is important to remember that general learning is intended to cultivate other intellectual virtues as well that have more to do with the nonscientific acquisition of recognitional and procedural knowledge. Among the more important instances of these kinds of knowledge are those that we need in order to be able to love God and our neighbor in the ways that, and to the extent that, God has created and called us to do. These sorts of knowledge involve not only our minds but also our hearts—including our will and our emotions. For instance, in order to love God well, we not only need to *acknowledge* the proposition that God deserves our love. We also need to *recognize* and *appreciate* humbly the majesty and grandeur of God (in contrast to our finitude and sinfulness) as we experience a relationship with God. And we need to *know how* to express our love to God in grateful worship. Moreover, in order to love our neighbor well, we not only need to *affirm* that he or she is created in God's image. We also need to *perceive* and *value* his or her worth as a fellow creature. And we need to *know how* to do what we can to foster his or her well-being.

This chapter has characterized general learning in such a way as to accommodate both the oratorical and the philosophical approaches. First, the nature of a general education is to cultivate human intellectual virtues. This may seem to favor the philosophers. However, as we will see later, among the intellectual virtues is *practical wisdom*, which has as its goal the living of a good and moral life. So this includes the oratorical emphasis as well as the philosophical. Second, we held up the pursuit and possible possession of truth as the primary goal of general learning. This allows for both the orators' relatively dogmatic assumption that we can *possess* the truth about *practical* matters as well as the philosophers' relatively skeptical claim that we should rather only *pursue* the truth about *speculative* matters. Third, we said the main methods of general learning are language-oriented. This characterization may diverge from some approaches, but it is congenial to both the orators and philosophers, who differ only in their different emphases concerning the *uses* of language. Finally, both orators and philosophers will agree with the general curriculum outlined here. Again, their differences involve the amount of stress to be placed on some academic disciplines as opposed to others.

These common commitments can coexist peacefully with the ongoing disagreements of a more specific sort that emerge out of the competing ideals of general learning. This continuing tension can be a good thing. Both the oratorical ideal and the philosophical ideal are prone to lapsing into degenerate forms. The oratorical ideal, with its focus on practicality, can become overly fixated on technology and technique at the expense of substance and content. It can also tend to become overly pragmatic, anti-intellectual, and antitheoretical. The philosophical ideal, which stresses theory, can become excessively pedantic, academic, and "ivory tower." It may become impractical, irrelevant, and removed from important human concerns. A healthy Christian general education will honor both of these ideals so that, in struggling to hold them together, the inadequate forms of each will be avoided. Perhaps the best way to do this is to make wisdom of all kinds (theoretical, practical, and productive) the primary goal of a Christian general learning.

A Note on Sources

In *Orators and Philosophers: A History of the Idea of Liberal Education*, expanded ed. (New York: The College Board, 1995), Bruce A. Kimball develops his distinction between the philosophical and oratorical ideals in the history of the liberal arts. The oratorical ideal finds its classical expression in Cicero's dialogue *De Oratore* (*On the Orator*). The philosophical ideal is manifested in Plato's many dialogues. A good example of the Socratic method can be found in Plato's dialogue *Euthyphro*, and Socrates expresses his attitude toward books (as opposed to conversations) in Plato's dialogue *Phaedrus*. Socrates distinguishes himself as a philosopher rather than a sophist in Plato's *Apology*. And Plato's emphasis on the pursuit of truth about speculative matters is expressed most fully in his *Republic*. Aristotle affirms his own version of this theme in *Nicomachean Ethics* (especially in book 10). In his *Rhetoric*, Aristotle attributes the claim to be able to "make the weaker argument into the stronger" to the sophist Protagoras. In *Cultivating Humanity: A Classical Defense of Reform in Liberal Education* (Cambridge: Harvard University Press, 1998), Martha C. Nussbaum employs the theme of the cultivation of humanity—from Seneca's *De Ira* (*On Anger*)—in her own account of liberal education. See Aristotle's *Nicomachean Ethics* for his discussion of human virtue or excellence as involving the actualization of human potential (and book 6 in particular for the actualization of our potential for intellectual virtue). In his *Aristotle for Everybody: Difficult Thought Made Easy* (New York: Macmillan, 1978), Mortimer Adler explains Aristotle's account of how we can cultivate and employ intellectual virtue in the form of theoretical, practical, and productive wisdom about truth, goodness, and beauty.

Questions for Reflection and Discussion

1. Are you attracted more to the oratorical ideal or to the philosophical ideal of the liberal arts? Why?

2. How can the orators and philosophers, in spite of their disagreements about the purpose of liberal learning, agree that a liberal education values truth and reason and is both general and humane? Explain.

3. Are you drawn to one type of wisdom (theoretical, practical, and productive) more than to the other two types? If so, why? If not, why not?

CHAPTER THREE

CHRISTIAN GENERAL LEARNING

We have defined learning in general as a natural process that results in a gain of knowledge. We have also characterized general learning as learning that is humane and primarily intellectual (in a broad sense of that word, that includes intellectual virtues that involve the heart as well as the mind—such as knowing how to love). What distinguishes *Christian* general learning? This chapter will identify four ways in which a Christian general education is distinctive. In an ideal Christian college or university, the addition of Christian theology will serve to (1) *complete*, (2) *ground*, (3) *correct*, and (4) *direct* general learning.

Four Aspects of Christian General Learning

First, Christian theology *completes* general learning. A general education is ideally not only general but also universal. That is, it should impart the knowledge and skills needed for human flourishing (general knowledge) and also expose students to all the major domains of human knowledge and investigation (universal knowledge). Since Christian theology constitutes an area of human knowledge and investigation, an ideal general education will be Christian. This is the sense in which Christian subjects *complete* a general education. In the previous chapter, we listed the academic disciplines that are typically included in a general learning curriculum—whether Christian or non-Christian. These disciplines are usually clustered into academic divisions such as the natural sciences, the social sciences, the formal sciences, and the humanities (including the arts). But theology does not properly belong in any of these divisions. The social science division will often offer courses in *comparative religion*, which make as objects of knowledge *what the adherents of different religious traditions believe.* But such courses don't treat any of these beliefs as *knowledge*. Only theology does. So if Christian theology is a source of knowledge, a curriculum that omits it is not universal and is therefore incomplete.

In *The Idea of a University*, the nineteenth-century Roman Catholic educator John Henry Newman argued that every university ought to teach theology. Here is his argument for this claim:

> Premise 1: A university, by definition, teaches "universal knowledge" (i.e., it teaches every subject that includes truths that can be known).
>
> Premise 2: Theology is a branch of knowledge—it is a subject that includes knowable truths.
>
> Conclusion: Therefore, a true university will teach theology.

Today, of course, many institutions of higher learning classified as "universities" exclude the teaching of theology from their academic programs. How should we think about Newman's argument in light of this educational reality? One response is to deny premise 2, the claim that theology is a branch of knowledge. This would allow a person consistently to claim that an institution can be a genuine university even if it excludes theology. This is, perhaps, the position of most educators today. Another reply is to deny premise 1 by defending the view that a university is not bound by its nature to teach all domains of knowledge. A skeptical, postmodern argument for this position might deny the very possibility of knowledge, and even truth. Supporters of this approach could say that a university could be unified around the common interests of its constituents, whatever those interests might be. A final position is to agree with Newman and conclude that contemporary secular "universities" are not *true* universities.

Whatever conclusion a person comes to about today's secular "universities" in light of Newman's argument, it seems undeniable that some form of his reasoning is inescapable when applied to Christian colleges and universities. Ideally, a general education will be an education in all academic areas in which important truths can be discovered. Since Christian theology is such an area of study, an ideal general education should include the study of Christian theology. From the standpoint of this argument, any general education that excludes the study of Christian theology is deficient. Moreover, as Newman points out, by its nature, Christian theology has an especially important role to play relative to the other academic disciplines. A cardinal Christian doctrine is that God is the sovereign creator of everything that exists other than God. Consequently, when we study any aspect of the universe, we are studying God's creation. Our studies provide us with both direct knowledge of the created order and indirect knowledge of God, the creator of this order. Another Christian belief is that the key to the redemption and fulfillment of the whole universe is to be found in God. Thus any discipline in which questions are raised about value, meaning, and purpose will be substantially crippled if Christian theology is not a part of the overall academic program that contains that discipline.

Second, Christian theology *grounds* general learning. The addition of Christian theology and other Christian studies does not merely make the list of academic disciplines longer. Instead, Christian general learning is learning from the standpoint or perspective of Christian faith. Christian learners should approach every learning situation asking,

"What should (or may) a Christian think about this?" Your Christian convictions provide a *ground* or foundation for learning. They are the starting point or basis on which you engage in the process of learning. They are the initial "given" of your learning experience. Now it is true that Christians will continue to learn about their faith as they take up Christian studies. Consequently, one's Christian perspective may be broadened. But what one believes may also be revised or corrected. The Christian convictions with which one begins the enterprise of general learning are really a *provisional* ground. To say that your convictions are a ground is to say that they are what one assumes to be settled as a basis for other beliefs one has. To say they are provisional is to say that one is open to the possibility that they are in need of amplification or correction. This can be a difficult balance to strike, but the very idea of Christian general learning requires that you find such a balance.

St. Augustine (354–430 CE): Faith grounds reason

- Experience-based faith in God can lead to theological understanding and knowledge through philosophical reasoning (argumentation) about God.

St. Thomas Aquinas (1225–1274 CE): Reason grounds faith

- Philosophical reasoning (argumentation) about God can lead to theological understanding and knowledge as a foundation for faith in God.

Christian convictions are the provisional ground of Christian general learning. What should ground Christian convictions themselves? The answer to this question has been the subject of much controversy throughout the history of Christian education. Roughly speaking, there are two main competing positions on this issue. Augustinians hold that faith is the ultimate ground of Christian belief. Their motto is "faith seeking understanding." Christian education, on their view, is a process of employing reason to work out the implications of Christian faith. Educators in the tradition of Thomas Aquinas (the Thomistic tradition), on the other hand, believe that Christian faith ought to be based on reason. In particular, one establishes the existence and main attributes of God on the basis of reason. This provides a rational foundation for one's acceptance of the truths of Scripture on the basis of faith. Christians continue to be divided on this issue. However, those who disagree about the ultimate ground of Christian belief can still agree that Christian convictions, whatever their basis, are the appropriate ground of general learning.

Third, Christian theology *corrects* general learning. Consistency requires that your beliefs be logically compatible. Accordingly, if a claim conflicts with something you believe to be true about the Christian faith, if you are logical, you will refrain from believing both things. In such a case, you may end up revising your Christian convictions. However, you may also end up rejecting the other claim. How it goes will depend on the claims in question. For instance, suppose you are watching Carl Sagan's television series *Cosmos*. Dr. Sagan comes on and says, "The cosmos is all that is, or ever was, or ever will be." Has Sagan said something true? Well, as a Christian, you believe that God created the universe. You assume that by "cosmos," Dr. Sagan means "universe." So if what he says is true, then God has never existed and never will, since God is not the universe or a part of it. Thus what Sagan said is inconsistent with a fundamental Christian belief. They can't both be true. In this case, the Christian belief is so basic that the only reasonable course open to you as a Christian learner is to conclude that Sagan is wrong. It is, however, sometimes appropriate in such circumstances to revise your Christian convictions instead. For instance, the Catholic Church condemned Galileo on the grounds that his thesis that the Earth moves is inconsistent with Scripture. (It conflicts, for instance, with a literal reading of Ps. 104:5 NIV: "He set the earth on its foundations; it can never be moved.") However, scientific investigation eventually confirmed that Galileo was correct. In this case, an assumption about the Christian faith had to be revised.

Why is it appropriate to side with Christian convictions in one instance but not in another? A comparison of these two examples illustrates one general principle that ought to govern Christian thinking in this area. In the first example, Carl Sagan, a scientist, makes a philosophical or religious claim without any arguments to back up his position. Christians can rightfully reject such an unwarranted claim and stick to their religious convictions. In the second example, the Church made an empirical scientific claim on the basis of a fallible interpretation of the Bible. The general lesson to be drawn here is that scientists should not make unwarranted theological or philosophical claims and Christians should be careful not to draw empirical scientific conclusions on the basis of inadequate biblical or theological grounds. More generally, when a theological or philosophical claim conflicts with an empirical scientific claim, one should opt for the claim for which one has a stronger rational basis. That is, one should accept the position for which one has better evidence or more reason to think it is true. An important part of Christian general learning is the formulation and justification of general methodological principles such as this that ought to govern one's thinking about the interplay between Christian studies and the other academic disciplines.

Fourth, Christian theology *directs* general learning. In Chapter One, we discussed knowledge as the goal of all learning, including knowing and understanding the truth, knowing how to recognize and classify things, and knowing how to perform a variety of skills (both intellectual skills and practical, moral skills). In Chapter Two, we suggested that the purpose of *general* learning is the acquisition of all the intellectual virtues that have truth, goodness, and beauty as objectives. Another way to put this is that the goal of general learning is to acquire the ability to use your mind well for the sake of knowing the truth, knowing how to live a good life, and knowing how to make beautiful and useful things.

Though this formulation does provide general learning with a purpose, it also leaves a number of important questions unanswered. Are some truths more important than others? That is, are some truths more worth knowing than others? If so, is there a way to distinguish the more valuable from the less valuable truths? What makes a life a good one? Is there one general way of living that is better than all the others? Is it possible to know what kind of life is best? Are some things really more beautiful than others are, or is beauty in the eye of the beholder? For which human purposes is it most worth producing useful things?

These questions can be answered adequately only from the standpoint of a relatively specific worldview that provides answers to perennial questions about reality, knowledge, and value. The Christian faith offers such a perspective. Christian theology provides general answers to all these questions (though many specific issues are the subjects of debate between Christian theologians). For instance, the good life can be defined in terms of knowing, loving, and serving God. The truths most worth knowing, the actions most worth taking, and the things most worth making will be those truths, actions, and things that contribute best to knowing, loving, and serving God.

In providing these relatively specific answers to the general questions about what is true, what is good, what is beautiful, and what is useful, Christian theology provides direction to general education. That is, Christian thinking about God enables us to home in on an accurate understanding of what is genuinely real, worthwhile, pleasing, and helpful—and such thinking serves this purpose by providing us with reasons to set aside alternative and competing specific answers to these general questions. Moreover, once we begin thinking about everything from a Christian perspective, our reflections from this vantage point can continue to direct us toward a fuller and more complete account of how things are, how things ought to be, how things ideally could be, and how we can make things better.

Can Theology and Philosophy Be Sciences?

St. Thomas Aquinas held that theology is the *noblest* science and that all the other sciences are subservient to it. His view is often phrased as the claim that theology is the "queen" of the sciences and that philosophy is its "handmaiden." So as far as he was concerned, theology is a science (in the broad sense of this word that we employed in the previous chapter). And to the extent that he thought philosophy could be used to assist in the pursuit of theological knowledge, it seems that he thought it a science too.

Theology is typically divided into the categories of natural and nonnatural (revealed) theology. Natural theology involves an attempt to gain knowledge about God in a way that requires human reason unaided by God's special revelation through Christ and in the Bible. An example of natural theology is the attempt to confirm that God is real (and to discern something about God's nature) by reasoning that the best explanation of the existence of the universe is that God exists as its creator. These exercises of human reason for this purpose are always at least partly philosophical and sometimes (as in the case of this example) also partly observational (empirical). So it's clear that one contribution of philosophy to theology is to provide an essential part of the means by which to do *natural* theology. Consequently, if natural theology is a science, then since natural theology is based on philosophy, philosophy (or at least *some* of philosophy) is a science too.

What about nonnatural, revealed theology—theology that focuses on the Bible? Revealed theology involves an attempt to acquire knowledge about God and God's will on the basis of testimony (rather than philosophical reasoning). We come to know things on the basis of someone's testimony that something is true by means of taking that person at his or her word. And we take people at their word when we trust that they are neither lying nor deceived. When we trust that someone is telling us the truth, we have faith in them—or at least in their authority with respect to the matter about which they are communicating to us. In the case of the Bible, we come to know things about God and God's will by trusting both the human authors of Scripture (through whom God speaks to us) and God. In short, we know that whatever the Bible teaches is true because it is God's word to us through its trustworthy human authors.

It is clear that theology and philosophy aspire to knowledge of truths about reality. After all, theology is the "study of God," and philosophy is the "love of wisdom." But it is widely believed today that neither of these academic disciplines is capable of yielding knowledge. So if a science, in our broad sense, is a means by which to arrive at propositional knowledge, then there is a general assumption at present that neither theology nor philosophy is a science.

Why is there such skepticism about theology and philosophy? Arguably, the main reason for these doubts involves the degree of disagreement over the answers to theological and philosophical questions and the perception that this disagreement is due to the lack of a method in these disciplines adequate to produce knowledge. It is important to say *degree* of disagreement here, since there is some disagreement in *all* the sciences about some of the truth claims that emerge in the process of engaging in those sciences. So the mere presence of disagreement does not disqualify an intellectual activity from counting as a science.

Is there enough disagreement about theological and philosophical claims to render them useless as means to acquire knowledge and thus impotent as sciences, and do these disciplines really lack a method sufficient for the attainment of knowledge? Arguably, the answer to both of these questions is "no." For one thing, the Bible affirms the possibility of our knowing some things about God and God's will (see, for instance, Prov. 9:10, Phil. 3:10–11, Luke 1:4, and 2 Peter 1:5). Also, in Romans 1:18–20, Paul explains why, though knowledge of God is available, it is not universally shared. Given what we said above, theology and philosophy are sciences if it is possible to come to know things about God through both exercising our reason and placing our trust in the authors (and Author) of the Bible. Arguably, it *is* possible for us to come to know things about God in these two ways—especially when we are achieving the goals of Christian general learning by becoming the right kind of person with the right sort of mind. So Christian theology and philosophy, at least in part, are both sciences—each of these disciplines is a source of knowledge.

The Goals of Christian General Learning

The Anglican theologian, literary critic, and novelist Harry Blamires says that the goal of Christian education is the formation of a "Christian mind." Christian philosopher Michael Peterson expands this idea to include the whole person. From his perspective, the total aim of Christian education is the formation of a Christian person. Human persons are, of course, more than just minds. We have hearts and bodies as well. We have desires and feelings in addition to thoughts. We can also act as well as think. Acting responsibly on the basis of our thoughts, feelings, and desires requires the cultivation of moral virtues in addition to intellectual virtues. We stated above that the goal of general learning is to cultivate the intellectual virtues—that is, those mental habits that enable you to use your mind well. Does this way of articulating the goal of general learning favor Blamires's narrower conception of Christian education over Peterson's more inclusive version? Not necessarily. There is a way to construe their views so as to make them compatible.

This harmonization requires us to make a distinction between three kinds of goals: *proximate* goals, *ultimate* goals, and *intermediate* goals. A proximate goal of a given activity is a goal one aims at *first* in undertaking that endeavor. It is the *immediate* goal of one's efforts. One can strive to achieve a proximate goal as a means to the attainment of other goals. If one of these other goals is a result one seeks to bring about for its own sake rather than for the sake of some further goal, it is an *ultimate* goal. Any goals one has that are neither proximate nor ultimate are *intermediate* goals. Proximate goals are often pursued for the sake of an intermediate goal or goals, and intermediate goals are desired for the sake of fulfilling other intermediate goals or an ultimate goal. An example will make these distinctions clear. Emma takes up a career in order to make money. Making money is Emma's proximate goal. The reason Emma wants to make money is so that she can be financially secure. This is an intermediate goal for Emma rather than an ultimate goal, since the reason she wants to be financially secure is so that she can be happy. Since Emma wants happiness only for its own sake, being happy is her ultimate goal.

We can now use these three kinds of goals to explain a way to combine consistently Blamires's conception of Christian education with Peterson's. Christian general learning is a goal-oriented activity. Ideally, students engage in general learning in order to actualize their intellectual potential. When this general learning is Christian, this involves learning to improve one's ability to "think Christianly," as Blamires puts it. However, this need not be the only goal of a Christian general education. An important intermediate goal of such an education is to become fully the kind of person that God made human beings to be. Intellectual virtue is at least a very important part of the means to this end. This is especially evident with respect to the various intellectual virtues that fall under the heading of "wisdom," as we will see throughout the rest of this book. Surely God intends for us to become both wise and good—both intellectual competence and morally good character are components of true godliness or "God-likeness." After all, God is both maximally intellectually able and supremely morally good. So general learning is for both the sake of mental growth (the proximate goal) and the growth of the whole person (the intermediate goal). This accommodates Peterson's position. But there is more (as both Blamires and Peterson would surely agree). Becoming a mature Christian person may be valuable in itself, but it is also a means to another goal that is good only in itself. This is the goal of glorifying God by knowing, loving, and serving God. This is the ultimate ideal goal of all human life and of each part of human life. Therefore, it is the ultimate ideal goal of the human activity of Christian general learning. So Christian general learning has three important goals: its proximate goal is to form Christian minds, its intermediate goal is to contribute to the cultivation of Christian personhood, and its ultimate goal is to enable people to glorify God by knowing, loving, and serving God. Students would do well to remember these three goals when they are working on an assignment, studying for an exam, or participating in a classroom conversation.

This account of the goals of Christian general learning provides a framework within which one may accommodate both the oratorical and the philosophical ideals discussed in the previous chapter. Recall that the oratorical ideal emphasizes the acquisition of the moral virtues for the sake of good living and good citizenship in the form of political involvement and contribution to the community. On this view, knowledge is good primarily as an instrument for these purposes, and effective speaking is the highest art. The philosophical view stresses the cultivation of the intellectual virtues for the sake of true believing and good scholarship focused on metaphysical and scientific investigation. On this view, knowledge is good primarily for its own sake, and logical thinking is the highest art. These two ideals are often in tension with each other, since their advocates tend to tout the values embodied in them as higher than those composing the other ideal. However, it is not necessary for these two visions for general education to be mutually exclusive. General learning can improve students' minds by making them wise. Wisdom is a kind of knowledge that comprises an important part of the proximate goal of a general education. Both orators and philosophers applaud it. This is because wisdom comes in a variety of forms. Wisdom includes knowledge of important truths. Valuable truths include those that explain the nature of reality and the meaning of human life, those that enable their possessors to live well, and those that provide a basis for making beautiful and useful things. A general education can instill wisdom of all these kinds. Though they stress different kinds of wisdom, orators and philosophers can agree that wisdom in general is a very good thing. Moreover, though these groups may highlight different aspects of the intermediate goal of a good life for human beings, they can both agree that wisdom is a very important component of such a life. Finally, if they are Christians, they can find much common ground in the commitment to the ultimate goal of glorifying God by knowing, loving, and serving God.

But as we have seen (in the Introduction), some Christians worry that striving to achieve the goals of general learning—whether characterized by the orators or defined by the philosophers—would be incompatible with attempting to realize the goals of Christian living, in spite of what we have argued to this point. We will now begin to address this concern.

A Note on Sources

John Henry Newman's *The Idea of a University* (Notre Dame: University of Notre Dame Press, [1852] 1982) contains his argument for the claim that every true university will teach theology. The Augustinian motto of "faith seeking understanding" is based on St. Augustine's saying "Believe, so that you may understand" (Augustine explains what he means by this saying in *Tractate* 29 [*Treatise* 29] on John 7:14–18) but is more fully developed in the work of the later Augustinian monk, philosopher, and theologian St. Anselm (see his *Proslogion*, which he originally entitled *Faith Seeking Understanding*). See Daniel L. Migliore's *Faith Seeking Understanding: An Introduction to Theology*, 3rd ed. (Grand Rapids: Eerdmans, 2014) for more on the Augustinian approach to theology (with a discussion of Aquinas as well). Carl Sagan's television program *Cosmos: A Personal Voyage* consisted of thirteen episodes that aired on PBS from September 28 to December 21, 1980. Excerpts can be seen on YouTube's "Carl Sagan's *Cosmos*" channel. See *The Church and Galileo*, edited by Ernan McMullin (Notre Dame: University of Notre Dame Press, 2005) for thirteen essays by international scholars about Galileo's interactions with the Roman Catholic Church. St. Thomas Aquinas's characterization of theology as the noblest science, with the other sciences (including philosophy) serving as its handmaidens, can be found in his *Summa Theologica*, part 1, question 1, article 5. See Dallas Willard's *Knowing Christ Today: Why We Can Trust Spiritual Knowledge* (New York: HarperOne, 2009) for further grounds for the claim that the Bible affirms the possibility of our knowing some things about God and God's will. Harry Blamires's discussion of the goal of Christian education as the formation of a Christian mind can be found in his *The Christian Mind: How Should a Christian Think?* (Ann Arbor: Servant Books, 1963). And Michael Peterson's alternative characterization of this goal in terms of the formation of a Christian *person* is contained in his *With All Your Mind: A Christian Philosophy of Education* (Notre Dame: University of Notre Dame Press, 2001).

Questions for Reflection and Discussion

1. Which of the four aspects of Christian general learning (general learning that Christian theology *completes*, *grounds*, *corrects*, and *directs*) do you think is most important? Why?

2. Do you agree that both Christian theology and (at least some of) philosophy are sciences (in the broad sense of this term)? Why or why not?

3. Are the proximate, intermediate, and ultimate goals of Christian general learning among your personal goals? If so, how important are they to you? If not, why not?

CHAPTER FOUR

SOCRATIC INQUIRY AND CHRISTIAN COMMITMENT

What does Jerusalem have to do with Athens? Absolutely nothing—at least as far as the early church father Tertullian was concerned. He was convinced that Christians should have nothing to do with Greek philosophies, that they should stick with the Bible alone. Many Christians both before him and after him have agreed. But a Christian general education is committed to showing that these fellow believers are wrong. What does Christian general learning have to do with Jerusalem and Athens? Absolutely everything. At the heart of this type of education is the integration of Christian faith and general learning.

Jerusalem, Athens, and "Faith Seeking Understanding"

But can Christian faith and general learning really be put together into a unified whole? Arguably, yes. But it's not easy to show how it can be done. Jerusalem and Athens are very different places with different emphases. These different emphases can seem at times to show that Tertullian was right—that Christian general learning is a contradiction in terms. However, if we think carefully—and philosophically—about these differences, we'll see that Tertullian was wrong. In making our case, we'll get some help from another early church father: St. Augustine.

It will help to remember one key similarity between Christian living and general learning: both aim at personal transformation. Both Christian churches and institutions dedicated to general education are in the business of making people better. They also agree that nothing less than the improvement of the whole person will do. This total personal change will affect our heads, our hearts, and our hands. But it is in getting down to specifics in this way that we begin to see the differences. When it comes to our heads, the general education emphasis is on critical thinking—on asking questions and keeping an open mind. The Christian emphasis is on conviction—on finding answers (to certain questions about God and human life) and sticking with them.

As we saw in Chapter Two, Socrates said that the unexamined life isn't worth living. He put this motto into practice by engaging his fellow citizens in critical conversations about their beliefs and values. His method was to ask a question and then subject proposed answers to criticism. Provisional and inadequate answers were then amended, and a new round of critical testing would begin. In this way, he hoped to show his contemporaries that they didn't really know what they thought they knew. He figured that people would never look for answers to important questions if they believed they already had them. Socrates was willing to admit that he was wise, but only in the sense that, unlike many of the people with whom he spoke, he knew that he didn't know much about the things that really matter. Even so, he never gave up seeking answers to his questions—though he never claimed to have found them. He was skeptical that we could ever know for sure the answers to important questions about life and the world. The Socratic method of critical questioning has been central in the general education tradition.

Jesus calls people to follow him (Matt. 4:19, Mark 1:17, and John 1:43). His teachings and parables continually confront his listeners with a decision. Examples include the following:

- No one can serve two masters (Matt. 6:24 and Luke 16:13).
- Whoever is not for Jesus is against him (Matt. 12:30 and Luke 11:23; see also Mark 9:40).
- Following Jesus requires giving him everything—including oneself (Matt. 10:39, Luke 9:24 and 14:33).

In *The Cost of Discipleship*, Dietrich Bonhoeffer famously said that when Christ calls a person, he bids that person come and die. There's a lot at stake here. Jesus does not expect blind obedience. He tells people to count the cost (Luke 14:28). But he does require the total commitment of those who have decided to be his disciples. He tells them not to look back when they start to plow (Luke 9:62). So following Jesus requires commitment, conviction, and closure. True Christian discipleship cannot be halfhearted and lukewarm. Jesus also says that he is the way, the truth, and the life (John 14:6).

Socrates and Jesus encourage us to use our heads in different ways: Socrates would have us constantly asking questions, but Jesus claims to be the answer. Many of us who have listened to both have sometimes felt ourselves pulled in opposite directions, and this inner feeling of being torn can be painful. It seems that the more open and questioning one is, the less one can be settled and confirmed in one's faith and in obedience to Christ. Too far in the critical direction threatens a loss of faith; too far in the direction of uncritical belief threatens a loss of intellectual integrity. What's a serious Christian student to do?

As mentioned earlier, St. Augustine wrestled with this issue. He found his solution in the motto "faith seeking understanding." The idea is that the foundation of one's search for knowledge, truth, and wisdom is one's faithful commitment to Christ, which arises out of one's experience of God's saving grace. Learning, then, becomes the means by which to deepen one's knowledge and understanding of God and creation. Education always takes place from the standpoint or perspective of Christian belief and conviction. This doesn't mean that the learner never questions his or her initial beliefs and values. But it does mean that these convictions are "innocent until proven guilty." The alternative approach is that one's fundamental beliefs and values are "guilty until proven innocent." This approach is both undesirable because it is paralyzing, and impossible; no one can live without at least provisional assumptions about what is true and right and good. So the Augustinian approach is to ask questions and seek answers from the standpoint of settled conviction—convictions that are, to some extent, open to correction, at least in their less central aspects.

What makes this Augustinian response to the tension between Jerusalem and Athens so powerful is that the Christian convictions that serve as the basis for our Socratic questioning are themselves rooted in a heart formed by various experiences of God's presence, power, provision, and love. And this heart formation yields a deep—and to some extent inexpressible—discernment of God and God's purposes (as revealed by God's Word and Spirit). This may well be what the seventeenth-century Augustinian mathematician, scientist, philosopher, and Christian apologist Blaise Pascal had in mind when he wrote, "The heart has reasons of which reason knows nothing" (Pensée #423). Moreover, the kind of community that can exist at a Christian college or university can provide a context for further experiences of God's transforming love. Such experiences, made possible by the practice of individual and communal spiritual disciplines of the sort we will discuss in Chapter Twelve, can provide Christian students with more faith-, hope-, and love-strengthening heart formation. And the results of such formation can enable them to engage in Socratic critical thinking with confidence and a sense of security rather than to spurn Athens and retreat fearfully to Jerusalem.

Christianity and Science: Creation and Evolution

One of the primary ways in which Christians today tend to side with Tertullian is in their attitude toward empirical science. Particularly in the United States, many conservative Christians are suspicious of scientific claims that appear to contradict what they believe the Bible teaches. Probably the main manifestation of this mistrust at the current time concerns the biological theory of evolution by natural selection rooted historically in the work of Charles Darwin. Since conservative Christians believe that the Bible is God's Word, they hold, correctly, that whatever the Bible teaches is true. Many of them also believe that the creation accounts in the first two chapters of Genesis teach us not only *that* God created the universe and all the things in it including human beings but also *how* God created these things.

Since the creation stories in those chapters portray God as creating human beings relatively immediately (i.e., in a relatively brief period of time) and directly (i.e., by means of a relatively simple process), it is natural to assume that God is using these stories to teach us that God employed these relatively short and simple means to create human beings. And if whatever God teaches us via the Bible is true, then it follows that it is true that God created humans in this relatively direct temporal and causal way. But if this is the truth about how God really created humans, then the scientific theory that humans evolved over a very long period of time by means of a complex process of natural selection cannot be true. So Christians who interpret these creation stories in this way believe that the scientific theory of evolution by natural selection must be rejected. Many non-Christians share this interpretation of Genesis and so agree with these Christians that creation and evolution are incompatible. But, of course, these non-Christians reject the Bible rather than the scientific theory of evolution. As a result, the Christians stay in Jerusalem, the non-Christians stay in Athens, and no efforts are made to build a road from one city to the other.

St. Augustine faced a similar problem in his day. He cautioned Christians not to interpret the Bible in ways that contradict what people have come to know about the world on the basis of observation and reasoning (empirical science). His primary concern is that Christians who do this will cause the non-Christians who hear them to deny important Christian doctrines as a result of having lost respect for the Scriptures that teach them. We can formulate the principle that Augustine has in mind here as follows: *Christians should never interpret the Bible in such a way as to contradict anything that is generally known to be true about the world on the basis of empirical science.*

There is good reason for all Christians to affirm this principle even if they disagree about how to apply it to the creation–evolution controversy. The reason we should endorse it is that whatever is known to be true on any basis (scientific or not) really *is* true. And if something is true, then whatever contradicts it has to be false. So if an interpretation of the Bible attributes to the Bible a claim that contradicts a known scientific truth, then that interpretation attributes a false claim to the Bible. But if the Bible is God's Word, then whatever it teaches is true. So if a particular interpretation results in the Bible saying something false, it cannot be a correct interpretation of something that the Bible teaches. Again, Christians can and should agree to accept this principle of biblical interpretation.

However, given the current state of the conversation among Christians about the creation–evolution controversy, Christians will disagree with each other about how to *apply* this principle to this debate. The focus of their disagreement will be on the question of whether the theory of evolution is generally known to be true on the basis of empirical scientific investigation. Special creationists (Christians who interpret the Genesis creation stories in such a way as to exclude the possibility that God created human beings by means of the process of evolution by natural selection) deny that the theory of evolution by natural selection is generally known to apply to the origin of the human species. Evolutionary creationists (Christians, also sometimes called "theistic evolutionists," who interpret the Genesis creation stories in such a way as to allow for the possibility that God created human beings by means of the process of evolution by natural selection) do not deny that the theory of evolution is generally known to apply to the origin of the human species. So these two groups can agree on the interpretive principle but disagree about its application to the Genesis creation accounts in light of the current creation–evolution debate.

There is another point of disagreement between special creationists and evolutionary creationists in addition to and separable from their debate about whether science has shown that the human species is a product of the process of evolution by natural selection. This is the difference of opinion, mentioned above, about the proper interpretation of the Genesis creation stories. Do those stories, when properly understood, exclude the possibility that God used evolution to create humans? If they do, then Christians really do have to choose between the Bible and contemporary science—at least insofar as science supports the biological theory of evolution. But if those narratives, when they are interpreted correctly, do not exclude the possibility of God's employment of the process of evolution to create humans, then Christians will not have to choose between the Scriptures and empirical science—regardless of whether the theory of evolution by natural selection turns out to be true.

But what is required for a correct understanding of the biblical creation stories? At a minimum, an interpretation of a passage of Scripture is appropriate only to the extent that it captures the *intentions* of the author of that passage. In the case of the Bible, the ultimate author is God, but of course God chose to reveal to us what God wants us to know through various human authors. So the best way to interpret a part of the Bible is, first of all, to discern the intentions of its human author in the context in which that author composed that passage, and second, to infer what God is teaching us through the writings of that human author. Let's call this interpretive principle "the principle of the primacy of authorial intention." In applying this principle to the Genesis creation stories, we need to ask whether the human author(s) (and ultimately the divine author) intended to tell us not only *who* created everything and *why* but also *how* this creator created everything and *how long* it took the creator to accomplish this task. And in answering these questions, we will need to take account of the original *context* in which the human author composed the work (time, place, audience, etc.) and also the *literary means* by which the author wrote it (style or genre). Both context and genre will help us figure out authorial intention.

We have now identified two questions Christians need to address in order to think responsibly about the creation–evolution debate:

1. Does the scientific theory of evolution by natural selection provide us with the true account of the biological origin of the human species?
2. Did the author(s) of the Genesis creation accounts intend to tell us how God created the universe and everything in it, including human beings?

Notice that the first question is an empirical scientific question that can be answered only by means of empirical scientific methods, and the second question is a theological question that can only be answered by means of rational hermeneutical (i.e., interpretive) methods. Notice also that special creationists will give a negative answer to question 1 and a positive answer to question 2, and evolutionary creationists will do the opposite in each case.

Let's return now to our contemporary Christian followers of Tertullian, who are suspicious of (or even reject) empirical science because of scientific theories that appear to them to conflict with the Bible (and the reason it seems to them that these theories contradict the Bible is that they are incompatible with how these Christians *interpret* the Bible). These are the Christians who identify with Jerusalem and want nothing to do with Athens. But now I hope it is clear that this isolationist position is irresponsible. Responsible Christians will seek to answer questions 1 and 2 stated in the previous paragraph as best they can. But the only reasonable way to investigate the answers to these two questions is by partaking in the nontheological Athenian disciplines of empirical science and philosophy. Answering 1 responsibly requires good scientific thinking about the theory of evolution, and answering 2 responsibly requires good philosophical thinking about how best to read the Bible. So there is no way that Christians can be intellectually responsible unless they are citizens of both Jerusalem and Athens.

Engaging in such a two-city process will involve an exercise of Socratic wisdom from the standpoint of Christian conviction. Or as an Augustinian following Anselm would put it, it would be an instance of faith seeking understanding. Since this search for understanding will be genuinely Socratic in nature, it will involve humbly engaging in both rational and critical thinking (both providing and then testing reasons for belief) in the pursuit of truth. Christians who participate in this intellectual journey as it applies to the creation–evolution debate may not know in advance how best to answer either the scientific or theological question with which they need to grapple to arrive at knowledge of the truth about how God created human beings. As we mentioned in Chapter Three in discussing the role of Christian convictions as correction, Christians may conclude that the claims of science need to be corrected on the basis of biblical considerations, or they may decide that they need to alter their interpretation of Scripture in light of their hermeneutical reflections and perhaps also their reading of scientific evidence. But regardless of where they end up—either as special creationists of some sort or evolutionary creationists of a certain type—they will have been responsible in employing their God-given minds in the search for wisdom about God's agency and human origins.

A Christian general education can provide excellent resources for an inquiry of this kind. The biblical and theological studies courses can help Christian students reflect carefully and critically about how best to think about God and God's Word. The natural science classes can equip them to think scientifically and critically about the biological theory of evolution by natural selection, and the philosophy courses can assist them in their rational and critical thinking about how best to interpret texts (including the Bible), how to reason about God and God's relation to the universe in light of God's revelation, how to evaluate scientific theories, and finally, how to think about the nature and limits of the empirical sciences and their relationship to other academic disciplines such as theology and philosophy itself.

Christianity and Science: The New Atheists

Ironically, the "New Atheists" comprise another group that agrees with Tertullian that Jerusalem and Athens should be kept separate, but unlike Tertullian, they favor Athens over Jerusalem. The New Atheists are a group of atheistic intellectuals who have published best-selling nonacademic books in the last ten years in which they (or most of them, anyway) argue or imply that religious believers are irrational and that religion is dangerous. Among the things that distinguish these "new" atheists from traditional atheists (such as Friedrich Nietzsche) are their use of science to justify their atheism and their appeal to morality apart from God to condemn religion and religious believers. But it is precisely their relatively uncritical acceptance of the possibility of morality without God and their largely unjustified application of science to the question of God's existence that make them subject to the charge of intellectual irresponsibility.

Christian students can be justifiably suspicious of the New Atheists' employment of human reason. For one thing, there is good reason to think that there are far better grounds for belief in God and much less reason to trust science to demonstrate God's nonexistence than the New Atheists are willing to acknowledge. On the one hand, the evidences for God include but go beyond what the empirical sciences can demonstrate about the world on the basis of observation of physical realities alone. On the other hand, by itself, empirical science does not have the power to determine that God does not exist, since the empirical sciences can study only physical things existing in nature and God is a supernatural, nonphysical being.

The New Atheists and others like them don't agree with these claims, because they assume either that the empirical sciences are the *only* source of knowledge ("*strong* scientism") or that these sciences are the *best* source of knowledge ("*weak* scientism"). People who accept either of these versions of scientism will conclude that we can't know that God exists unless there is adequate empirical scientific evidence for God. Their thesis that we can't know there is a God follows given the further assumption that there isn't adequate empirical scientific reason to think that God exists. Moreover, if they add the assumption (as many of them do) that if there were a God, there would be adequate scientific evidence for the reality of such a being, they can also infer that there is no God. This additional step turns their argument from a case for agnosticism (the view that we don't or can't know whether or not there is a God) into a basis for atheism (the claim that there is no God).

But why should we think that either version of scientism is true? There are good reasons to think that empirical science is not the only source of knowledge and that some other sources can be better than empirical scientific sources are—at least about certain things. For instance, the New Atheists' case for their claim that religion is a source of moral evil is based on their assumption that we have moral knowledge—that we can know that religion is morally bad and that the world would be a morally better place without it. But moral knowledge has a completely different source than empirical scientific knowledge has. Moral knowledge tells us what ideally should or ought to be the case, and empirical scientific knowledge can tell us only what actually is the case. That is, moral claims are normative and prescriptive, and empirical scientific claims are nonnormative and descriptive. Moreover, at least some of our moral knowledge is arguably more secure than all our empirical scientific knowledge. Though we cannot conceive of a situation in which it would be morally permissible to torture human infants just for the fun of it, we can at least imagine a possible circumstance in which a physical object resists conformity with the law of gravitation. Finally, ironically, scientism itself is not a scientific claim about the empirical world but a philosophical claim about the requirements for knowledge. So if at least *strong* scientism were true, it wouldn't be possible to know that it is true (because strong scientism entails that only statements confirmable by empirical science are knowable, and strong scientism is not a statement confirmable by empirical science).

In addition, the New Atheists' assumption that morality is possible in a godless world is problematic. Though it is clearly the case that atheists can and do have moral knowledge and that atheists can behave morally, it is not so clear that atheists can explain where morality comes from, how moral knowledge is possible, or why we should be moral. Christians have answers to each of these questions: morality is rooted in the will and character of God, God communicates his moral will to us by means of our consciences and the Bible, and we should live moral lives because doing so is the means by which we can love our creator and fellow human beings. The best atheistic answers to these questions are based on an appeal to evolution by natural selection. But arguably, a morality based on natural selection alone can promote only whatever is conducive to the "survival of the fittest," and so will ultimately fall short of the moral ideals needed to ground the New Atheists' arguments.

This brief response to the New Atheists does not settle the debate they have started. But it does illustrate the way in which students engaged in Christian general learning can think rationally and critically about the assumptions underlying their claims. More generally, this discussion of the questionable nature of the New Atheists' presuppositions and reasoning highlights the importance of keeping the limits of human reason in mind. Athens simply doesn't have the intellectual resources adequate to show that we can and should disregard Jerusalem (just as Jerusalem doesn't have the intellectual resources adequate to show that we can and should disregard Athens—as the previous section showed). Genuinely wise people will draw from both Jerusalem and Athens in order to further their wisdom.

A Note on Sources

Tertullian's query, "What does Jerusalem have to do with Athens?" occurs in chapter 7 of his *De Praescriptione Haereticorum* (*On the Prescription against Heretics*). Plato records Socrates's statement that "the unexamined life isn't worth living" in his *Apology*, 38a. Dietrich Bonhoeffer wrote, "When Christ calls a man, he bids him come and die" in *The Cost of Discipleship* (London: SCM Press, [1948] 2001), 44. The Augustinian motto "faith seeking understanding" is based on Augustine's admonition to "believe, so that you may understand," which he discusses in *Tractate 29* (*Treatise 29*) on John 7:14–18. Blaise Pascal's reflection that "the heart has reasons of which reason knows nothing" can be found in his *Pensées*, trans. A. J. Krailsheimer (London: Penguin Books, 1966), 154 (Pensée #423). Charles Darwin develops his theory of evolution by natural selection in *On the Origin of Species*, published in 1859. Augustine's caution to Christians not to interpret the Bible in ways that contradict what people have come to know about the world on the basis of science can be found in his book *The Literal Meaning of Genesis*, chapter 19. E. D. Hirsch defends the principle of the primacy of authorial intention in *Validity in Interpretation* (New Haven: Yale University Press, 1967). The "New Atheists" include Sam Harris, the author of *The End of Faith: Religion, Terror, and the Future of Reason* (New York: Norton, 2004); Richard Dawkins, who wrote *The God Delusion* (Boston: Houghton Mifflin Harcourt, 2006); Christopher Hitchens, who penned *God Is Not Great: How Religion Poisons Everything* (New York: Twelve Press, 2006); and Daniel Dennett, whose book is *Breaking the Spell: Religion as a Natural Phenomenon* (New York: Penguin Books, 2007). Friedrich Nietzsche's articulations of atheism are located in works of his such as *Thus Spoke Zarathustra* (1883), *Beyond Good and Evil* (1886), and *The Antichrist* (1888).

QUESTIONS FOR REFLECTION AND DISCUSSION

1. In your approach to Christian general learning, do you lean more toward Jerusalem or more toward Athens? Do you think Augustine's "faith seeking understanding" provides a promising way to be a citizen of both of these cities? Why or why not?

2. Do you agree that "there is no way that Christians can be intellectually responsible unless they are citizens of both Jerusalem and Athens"? Why or why not? How would you answer the scientific question about the theory of evolution and the theological question about the proper way to read the Genesis creation stories?

3. How do you think the New Atheists could respond to the case made in this chapter for the claim that their atheism is based on intellectually irresponsible arguments?

SECTION TWO

WISDOM

CHAPTER FIVE

WISDOM IN THE GREEK TRADITION

LEARNING BETTERS THE MIND. GENERAL LEARNING YIELDS ALL-purpose mental improvement in the form of intellectual virtues. Christian general learning produces a *Christian* mind fit for valuable general thinking from a Christian perspective. Such thinking is aimed at the acquisition of wisdom. Both biblical and nonbiblical sources agree that wisdom is the most honorable intellectual virtue. What is wisdom? Is it the same as knowledge? If not, is it a kind of knowledge or something completely different? Is it the sort of thing that can be taught and learned? In this chapter, we will draw on the classical Greek tradition, and in the following two chapters, we will make use of the biblical tradition and two Asian traditions to address these questions.

Socrates, Plato, and Aristotle

As mentioned in the previous chapter, Socrates cross-examined his contemporaries in search of a genuinely wise person. He came to the paradoxical conclusion that he was wiser than they were in the sense that, unlike them, he knew that he wasn't wise. Thus Socrates considered himself not to be a *possessor* of wisdom, though he dedicated his life to the *pursuit* or *love* of wisdom. This made him a *philosopher* (a lover and seeker of wisdom) as opposed to a *sage* (a finder and possessor of wisdom). Socrates did not identify wisdom with knowledge. While he claimed to be unwise, he also claimed to know many things. Moreover, he was willing to grant that many people he questioned knew some things. So on Socrates's view, not all knowledge yields wisdom. On the other hand, he did think of wisdom as a form of knowledge. When he set out to find a wise person, he conversed with those who had a reputation for wisdom to see what they *knew*. So Socrates believed that some knowledge constitutes wisdom. What knowledge is this? A clue can be found in the main questions Socrates asked his interlocutors. These questions were primarily about matters Socrates considered very important: piety, virtue, justice, knowledge, courage, life, and death. They were questions about what makes life most worth living. They were also questions Socrates believed none of his fellow citizens could answer satisfactorily. Thus, in saying that no one was genuinely wise, Socrates was saying that no one knew enough about the things that matter most.

His student Plato showcased wisdom as the highest virtue. For him, wisdom consisted in knowledge of transcendent, eternal, and unchanging truths about important things like reality, goodness, and beauty. Plato believed that a wise person would know what was truly good in the most general sense. He thought wisdom was acquired by means of a lengthy and arduous process of education culminating in rigorous philosophical dialogue. In his ideal form of government, philosopher-kings and -queens who had been educated in this way would rule wisely and benevolently. Plato despaired of there ever being such ideal monarchs. However, he offered his principle that both individuals and states ought to be ruled by wisdom as a goal toward which to aim. Healthy people and institutions are guided by knowledge of what is worthwhile, valuable, and important. They have the courage to put this knowledge into practice and the discipline to refrain from thinking and acting unwisely. In short, wise rule breeds harmony and well-being. Thus, like his mentor, Plato believed that wisdom is knowledge of what is really good (beneficial, worthwhile, important, and valuable).

Plato's pupil Aristotle agreed with him that wisdom, generally speaking, involves knowledge of important truths. Aristotle also followed Plato in classifying wisdom as a virtue or excellence of the human mind or soul. Like Plato, he believed that human beings are born with the capacity to improve and excel in various ways that contribute to human well-being. On the basis of these shared ideas, Aristotle developed a more sophisticated account of human psychology. For one thing, Aristotle made a distinction between moral improvement and intellectual development. Our characters improve as we cultivate moral virtues like justice, courage, and self-control. Our minds improve as we acquire intellectual virtues like knowledge and wisdom. Aristotle believed that general human excellence requires both moral and intellectual virtue. Moreover, he held wisdom to be a prominent intellectual virtue. Actually, the English word "wisdom" is used to translate more than one Greek word used by Aristotle to denote an excellence of the mind. His recognition of different kinds of wisdom is a further improvement of the thinking of Socrates and Plato. In what follows, we will distinguish three kinds of wisdom characterized by Aristotle: *theoretical* wisdom, *practical* wisdom, and *productive* wisdom. Each kind of wisdom is a significant part of the overall intellectual virtue or excellence of mind that comprises the proximate goal of Christian general learning.

The Varieties of Wisdom

Aristotle used the Greek word *sophia* for *theoretical* wisdom, which is the culmination of theoretical *knowledge*. This type of knowledge—also called speculative knowledge ("*episteme*")—is knowledge of the fundamental explanatory principles of reality. Aristotle distinguished three distinct theoretical disciplines: "first philosophy" (the most foundational kind of philosophy, which includes theology and metaphysics), mathematics, and natural science. Aristotle's limitation of theoretical knowledge to these areas reflects his agreement with Plato that there is a kind of wisdom that involves only eternal and unchanging truths (though he recognized that the principles of the natural sciences do not hold with strict necessity). Knowledge acquired on the basis of these sciences is theoretical when it is knowledge acquired only for its own sake and not for the sake of practicality or utility. Today, scientists distinguish between pure and applied research. Scientists engage in *pure* research just for the sake of furthering our knowledge. The goal of *applied* research is to gain knowledge that can be put to use for practical purposes. In Aristotelian terms, the end of pure research is theoretical knowledge. One of the aims of applied research is what we will call "productive" wisdom, which we will discuss below. Though Aristotle included only the natural sciences among the disciplines that yield empirical theoretical knowledge, it seems appropriate to include the social sciences in this category as well. These latter sciences are theoretical disciplines when they are practiced purely for the sake of knowledge and understanding about individual and collective human thought and behavior of various kinds.

Theoretical knowledge becomes theoretical *wisdom* when the knower attains a mastery of the most important truths about speculative matters. Such an understanding of reality as a whole and in its various particular dimensions would constitute a *worldview*. We will have more to say about worldviews in Chapters Nine and Twelve. To the extent that people possess theoretical wisdom about something, they no longer need to strive for the truth about that subject matter. They are instead in a position to enjoy the contemplation of this truth (perhaps you have had a hint of this sort of experience when you have come to understand a concept, idea, or theory more fully). However, the human intellectual condition makes the ideal state of *complete* theoretical wisdom beyond our reach. We can agree with Socrates at least about *this* cognitive limitation. The intellectual virtue of theoretical wisdom is, however, a goal toward which we can strive and hope to attain to at least a partial extent.

Aristotle employed the Greek word *phronesis* for *practical* wisdom. Sometimes the English word "prudence" is used to translate this word. Practical wisdom includes knowledge of important truths about how to live a good life. But it is more than that. Aristotle believed there is an important relationship between practical wisdom and moral living. He thought that a person couldn't excel morally without practical wisdom. He also believed that a person couldn't have practical wisdom without being morally good. The reason for this close connection between practical wisdom and moral goodness is that practical wisdom includes not only knowledge of what is genuinely good for human beings but also a love for this good and an effective pursuit of it by behaving in good ways. Consequently, practically wise people must not only be able to deliberate effectively about what is good to do; they must also desire to do what is good and try to do it. Only a morally good person would consistently have such a desire. We can sum up the essence of practical wisdom by saying that a practically wise person is a person who is skilled in the art of living well. Such a person knows how to live the good life. This skill involves knowledge of truths about human nature and the meaning of human life. This knowledge enables its possessor to know what kind of human life is best and also how to go about living that life. That is, it is knowledge of both the ultimate end of life and the means to achieve that end. Thus the practical knowledge component of practical wisdom is knowledge for the sake of action rather than knowledge for its own sake. This is what distinguishes practical from theoretical wisdom.

When people use the word "wise" today to describe someone, they typically mean to attribute practical wisdom to that person. Someone with a lot of theoretical knowledge might instead be called "insightful." Even so, it seems appropriate to use the word "wisdom" to label each of these intellectual virtues. What they have in common is knowledge of important truths. They differ only in the ends to which these truths are put. In the case of theoretical wisdom, the end is contemplation. In the case of practical wisdom, the end is living well. There is another kind of knowledge in addition to theoretical and practical knowledge that it seems appropriate to call a kind of wisdom. This is *productive* knowledge.

Productive knowledge involves knowledge of truths about how to make things that have a valuable characteristic, such as beauty or utility. But like practical wisdom, productive wisdom is also more than just knowledge of truths. It is also an art or skill, and its possession requires a track record of having exercised this art or skill. Just as practical wisdom is both knowing the truth about what kind of life is best and knowing how to live such a life, productive wisdom is both knowing truths about the objects that are worth making and also having the ability to make these objects on the basis of a grasp of these truths. Aristotle called this intellectual virtue *techne*. This word is often translated as "skill" or "art." The reason it seems appropriate to call it a kind of wisdom is that it involves knowledge of important truths that can be employed in the production of worthwhile objects. We often say of people who are skilled in a particular area that they are "wise about" that area. For instance, a physician may be wise about the use of certain medications, and a writer may be wise about how to express her thoughts. When people are wise about a particular domain, we say that they have *expertise* in that area. They are experts at what they do. They are wise in the ways of plying their trade, executing their skill, or practicing their art.

Based on this survey of Greek philosophers, especially Aristotle, it seems reasonable to say that there are at least these three kinds of wisdom. What is the relationship between these kinds of wisdom and the kinds of knowledge discussed in Chapter One? Recall that in the process of defining learning, we distinguished propositional, recognitional, and procedural knowledge. These kinds of knowledge differ in their objects—they are distinguished in terms of what they are *about*. Propositional knowledge is about truths, recognitional knowledge is about concepts, and procedural knowledge is about procedures. What distinguishes each kind of wisdom—theoretical, practical, and productive—is their *purpose, end, or goal*. The goal of theoretical knowledge is contemplation of important speculative truths, the goal of practical knowledge is to live a good life, and the goal of productive knowledge is to make worthwhile (useful and/or beautiful) objects.

The following lists provide examples of each of the three kinds of knowledge in each of the three categories of wisdom. Clearly, each kind of wisdom is both complex and important.

Theoretically wise people

- know the truth about important speculative matters (propositional knowledge)
- can sort things into different conceptual categories (recognitional knowledge)
- know how to reason about logical relationships between propositions (procedural knowledge)

Practically wise people

- know the truth about what kind of human life is best (propositional knowledge)
- are able to distinguish a good action from a bad one (recognitional knowledge)
- know how to act in such a way as to live a good life (procedural knowledge)

Productively wise people

- know truths about what makes objects beautiful and useful (propositional knowledge)
- can distinguish a well-made object from a poorly constructed one (recognitional knowledge)
- know how to make worthwhile (beautiful and useful) objects (procedural knowledge)

We have seen that practical wisdom and productive wisdom are not purely intellectual but also involve appropriate desires and effective actions. Theoretical wisdom is not merely cognitive either. All three types of wisdom also have an important affective or attitudinal component. Theoretical wisdom involves the *enjoyment* of knowing important truths. Practical wisdom carries with it *zeal* to pursue the best kind of life. Productive wisdom incorporates an *appreciation* for what is useful and beautiful.

In short, each kind of wisdom is characterized by a love for something that is worthy of that love: truth in the case of theoretical wisdom, goodness in the case of practical wisdom, and beauty (and utility) in the case of productive wisdom. A good general education, then, will not only provide students with learning opportunities of various kinds, but it will also cultivate in them a love of learning and a love of the valuable things toward which their learning directs them. Most importantly, an ideal *Christian* general education will enable students to learn not only to think Christianly and to love doing so but also to better love the One who is the source of all learning, truth, goodness, and beauty. And the more students love and revere God, the more they will be in a position to become wiser. After all, the beginning of wisdom is the fear of the Lord (Ps. 111:10).

Multiculturalism, Relativism, and Postmodernism

As we will see in the next two chapters, the ancient Greek tradition to which Socrates, Plato, and Aristotle contributed is not the only potential source for Christian general thinking about the nature and varieties of wisdom. Both the Judeo-Christian tradition contained in the Bible and various other world traditions, including Asian traditions, can provide resources for our thinking about wisdom as well. The existence of these alternative traditions for our purposes means that Christian general learning can be *multicultural.*

However, a proponent of Christian general education will not necessarily endorse every version of multicultural*ism*. Multiculturalism, when contrasted with traditionalism, is the view that a curriculum consisting primarily in the works of white European males based on a combination of the Greco-Roman and Judeo-Christian traditions should not dominate educational programs. Multiculturalists believe, rightly, that other cultural expressions are worthy of study as well. *Christian* multiculturalists advocate studying the diverse products of *all* cultures on the grounds that they are produced by people made in God's image. Christian multiculturalists also resist the privileging of any human cultures in such a way as to suggest they are entirely superior to other human cultures. But many multiculturalists also think that the mere traditionalist emphasis on the products of (often dead) white male Europeans automatically has the effect of marginalizing and even oppressing people who are nonwhite, non-European, or female. Many of those who hold this view advocate a multicultural curriculum for political purposes. The political agenda they seek to introduce into the curriculum is often called "identity politics."

Identity politics is an effort to promote the interests of a certain group of people by means of fostering recognition of the group's identity. Those engaged in this enterprise often do not allow any sort of critical evaluation of this group. Such assessment is banned on the grounds that it makes illegitimate appeal to evaluative standards that are alleged to be foreign to the group being criticized. This claim is based on the grounds that all evaluative standards or norms are relative. This normative relativism is then justified by descriptions of ways in which different cultures, societies, and groups differ in beliefs, values, and practices. For instance, anthropologists will point out that different cultures have different ideas about what makes something beautiful or what makes conduct morally right. It is then concluded on the basis of these descriptive, factual, social scientific grounds that what really is beautiful and what really is morally right are relative to specific cultures. That is, it is concluded that there is no such thing as one absolute and objective standard of beauty or goodness. Many multiculturalists also subscribe to a more radical kind of relativism that denies the existence of one absolute or universal and objective *truth about the way things really are*. This thoroughgoing relativism about truth, goodness, and beauty is the hallmark of an influential version of contemporary postmodernism. It is the kind of multicultural approach to education that is based on this kind of postmodernism that cannot be incorporated into a Christian general education.

Why should Christian general learning shun radically relativistic postmodernism? The primary reason is that this latter approach undercuts the very foundation of both the Christian faith and traditional general learning. Traditionally, a general education has consisted in the pursuit of wisdom about what is true and good and beautiful. Though opinions have differed about the extent to which such wisdom can be attained, educators of general learners have agreed that if it could be achieved, it would be the same for all learners, at least in general respects. According to Christian theology, the most important truths about reality are that God exists, that God created everything else that exists, and that God the Son, the second person of the Holy Trinity, became incarnate as Jesus of Nazareth for the sake of providing atonement for the sins of the world. Christians believe that these truths are universal and objective. That is, they believe that they are the same for everyone regardless of the time and place at which they live and that they correspond to the way things really are.

This is not to say, of course, that everyone *believes* or *accepts* these truths. It also does not mean that they are self-evident, obvious, or otherwise easy to believe. Moreover, to claim that these are absolute and objective truths is not necessarily to claim any special insight into the nature of reality or to be intellectually arrogant. The (hopefully humble) claim is simply that these things are an important part of the truth about the way things really are—even if they are not universally accepted. The same sort of thing can be said about goodness. Perhaps no one is in a position to know the complete nature of moral goodness with complete accuracy. However, Christians share with many others the opinion that whatever moral goodness amounts to, it is the same for all people in all times and places. This is not to say, of course, that it is easy to figure out what is good and right, especially in controversial matters. It is also not to say that general moral principles ought always to be applied in the same way in every culture. People in every culture should hold their moral opinions with degrees of confidence appropriate to the content of these opinions. They should also be humble, open to correction, and tolerant of many of the convictions of those who disagree with them. And they should look for points of moral agreement by exploring the extent to which apparent moral disagreement is really just a difference of opinion about the facts. All of this can be so while maintaining that the general moral will of God for humankind is invariant across cultures.

Finally, though there is more disagreement over the extent to which judgments of *beauty* are nonrelative and nonsubjective, Christians have grounds for thinking that there is an objective basis for distinguishing what is beautiful from what is not. If something is really beautiful, then there is something about the way that thing is, in and of itself, that is genuinely admirable. Moreover, something is worthy of our admiration only to the extent that it reflects the divine nature—that is, only insofar as it is like God, who is the source of all things bright and beautiful. There is, then, a general standard to which Christians can appeal in making aesthetic judgments, even if it is difficult to know for sure whether these judgments are adequate to this standard.

So Christians have reasons for affirming the existence of the true, the good, and the beautiful and for rejecting radical or extreme postmodern views that relativize these to different cultures. Christian general learning is then the search for wisdom about this triad of valuable ends—wherever this wisdom can be found. However, some Christians are reluctant to agree that much in the way of wisdom about truth, goodness, and beauty can be found in non-European cultures and non-Christian traditions. Others allow for this possibility but hesitate to affirm foreign insights unless they are also clearly present at home as well. Extreme versions of this attitude of intellectual isolationism involve the kind of ethnocentrism against which many postmodernists react in the name of tolerance and appreciation. But modernist ethnocentrism and postmodernist multiculturalism are equally objectionable from a Christian standpoint. They are intellectually, morally, and aesthetically bankrupt. Adherents of the former viewpoint are often unjustifiably elitist, dogmatic, and arrogant about the superiority of their knowledge of what is true, good, and beautiful. Proponents of the latter are excessively relativistic, as we have seen. This relativism actually backfires on them, since it leaves them with no basis on which to find what is really true, good, and beautiful in *any* culture. Some may want to affirm the superiority of non-Western over Western cultures in some respects. Others may deny the relative superiority of any culture over another, even in limited respects, and yet still want to insist that each culture ought to be appreciated for its valuable components. However, it is not legitimate for relativistic postmodernists to make these kinds of evaluative claims, since these claims presuppose evaluative standards that are external to the culture being evaluated. Christian general learners should take the middle road between these two extremes. This middle road consists in a humble openness to finding wisdom in other cultures (and even other religions) together with a conviction that true wisdom is a matter of conformity to standards of truth, goodness, and beauty that transcend all cultures. This intellectual pilgrimage is fraught with dangers (such as excessive dogmatism at one extreme end of the spectrum and excessive skepticism at the other). However, it is a journey that is well worth taking.

Let us turn now to see what the Bible says about wisdom and then consider how the biblical perspective on wisdom compares with the classical Greek conception sketched above. Following that, we will look to some non-Western and nonbiblical Asian traditions in an attempt to broaden and deepen our understanding and appreciation of the nature and varieties of wisdom.

A Note on Sources

Plato's *Apology* is the dialogue in which Socrates relates his quest to find a genuinely wise person by questioning those who had a reputation for wisdom. Plato formulates his view of wisdom as knowledge of transcendent, eternal, and unchanging truths most fully in his

Republic (see especially books 7 and 8). Aristotle discusses his view of wisdom in *Nicomachean Ethics*, book 6, and we are following Mortimer Adler's *Aristotle for Everybody: Difficult Thought Made Easy* (New York: Macmillan, 1978) in distinguishing the three kinds of wisdom characterized by Aristotle (theoretical, practical, and productive). Aristotle also analyzes the relationship between practical wisdom and good living in *Nicomachean Ethics*. In *Cultivating Humanity: A Classical Defense of Reform in Liberal Education* (Cambridge: Harvard University Press, 1998), Martha C. Nussbaum develops a version of multiculturalism that does not entail the varieties of identity politics, postmodernism, and relativism that we have urged Christians to avoid. For general explanatory and critical discussions of postmodernism from a Christian point of view, see Stanley Grenz's *A Primer on Postmodernism* (Grand Rapids: Eerdmans, 1996) and Douglas Groothuis's *Truth Decay: Defending Christianity against the Challenges of Postmodernism* (Downers Grove: InterVarsity Press, 2000).

Questions for Reflection and Discussion

1. Do you agree with Socrates, Plato, and Aristotle that wisdom, as they understand it, is a great good that is worth pursuing above many other things? Why or why not?

2. Which of the three kinds of wisdom (theoretical, practical, and productive) do you think you need to focus on the most, if any? Why?

3. Do you agree that Christian general learning should shun radically relativistic postmodernism and the type of multiculturalism that is based on it? Why or why not?

CHAPTER SIX

WISDOM IN THE BIBLICAL TRADITION

THOUGH THE THEME OF WISDOM IS SCATTERED THROUGHOUT THE Old Testament, only three books in this collection qualify as works of "wisdom literature." These are the books of Job, Proverbs, and Ecclesiastes. Biblical scholars differ over exactly what it is that distinguishes wisdom literature from other literary genres employed by the writers of Scripture. However, it seems reasonable that one theme that unites these wisdom books is guidance in the search for knowledge and understanding amid theoretical and practical perplexity, problems, and puzzles. These works contain observations, lessons, and instructions about what thoughts, attitudes, and actions are appropriate for a person attempting to live wisely in God's world. From Job's search for justice and understanding in the midst of his undeserved pain and suffering, we learn about the limits of human understanding and the sufficiency of God's presence during trial. From the admonitions, maxims, and exhortations contained in Proverbs, we learn about the benefits of putting God-given wisdom into practice and the perils of failing to do so.

From the writer of the book of Ecclesiastes, who offers the teaching of the pessimistic "Teacher" to his son for critical consideration, we learn that the search for wisdom must be conducted on the basis of fearing and obeying God. It is important to recognize both the diversity and the unity of these biblical viewpoints about wisdom. Let us consider the book of Job first.

Wisdom in Job, Proverbs, and Ecclesiastes

The book of Job starts with a prose folktale in which, in a conversation with God, the "Accuser" predicts that the pious and righteous Job would curse God if he were to lose his wealth. However, Job continues to bless God even after God allows the Accuser to render Job poor and childless. The Accuser then afflicts Job with a skin ailment, but Job still refrains from cursing God. At this point, a conversation ensues between Job and three friends who come to comfort him but end up challenging him. The poetic passage that records their discussion contains three rounds of dialogue between Job and each of his three friends. These friends agree that Job's suffering is a just consequence of his wrongdoing. Job counters by insisting that his innocence makes his calamities undeserved. This interchange culminates in Job's challenge to God to answer him. At this point, a new person, Elihu, enters the conversation. He "was angry at Job because he justified himself rather than God," and he "was angry also at Job's three friends because they had found no answer, though they had declared Job to be in the wrong" (Job 32:2–3 NRSV). Elihu accuses Job of adding "rebellion to his sin" (34:37 NRSV) and warns that God "does not regard any who are wise in their own conceit" (37:24b NRSV). Finally, God answers Job out of a whirlwind. However, God does not explain or justify Job's suffering but rather challenges Job to explain or justify his self-righteous condemnation of God. In doing so, he contrasts his sovereignty over creation with Job's creaturely limitations. Job's response is to repent of his ignorant insolence. The book of Job concludes with a short prose section in which God chastises Job's friends for their folly ("you have not spoken of me what is right, as my servant Job has done" [42:8 NRSV]) and restores Job's fortunes twofold.

If the book of Job poses the age-old question "Why do bad things happen to good people?" it doesn't so much answer it as much as place it in proper perspective. This perspective is mostly practical and moral but also somewhat theoretical and intellectual. The limited theoretical insight of the book is that human beings are not in a position to explain or justify God's allowing undeserved suffering. Indeed, a chapter of Job placed right before Job's final defense contains a hymn on the inaccessibility of wisdom. In answer to the question "Where shall wisdom be found?" (28:12 NRSV), the reply is that "mortals do not know the way to it, and it is not found in the land of the living" (28:13 NRSV). However, "God understands the way to it and he knows its place" (28:23 NRSV). The idea here is that human beings cannot find wisdom by themselves but must rely on God to provide them with however much of it he chooses to give them. And how much is this? Though God "looks to the ends of the earth and sees everything under the heavens" (28:24 NRSV) and could therefore grant us with a rich supply of theoretical or speculative wisdom, what he actually reveals about wisdom to human beings is limited to practical matters: "And he said to humankind, 'Truly, the fear of the Lord, that is wisdom; and to depart from evil is understanding'" (28:28 NRSV).

The moral admonition implied by the book is connected to its theoretical observation. It is that our ignorance of God's purposes makes it inappropriate for us to condemn God for allowing suffering. Though Job's suffering may have been undeserved, he erred in relying on his own judgment instead of humbly fearing the Lord. Importantly, Job's initial folly was not necessarily to proclaim his innocence. He may well have had ample experiential evidence of his relative goodness. His mistake was instead to question God's justice. However, the way of wisdom is not to justify the ways of God by finding fault with the sufferer either. This is the approach taken by Job's three friends that God rejected ("you have not spoken of me what is right" [42:8 NRSV]).

What we learn from the book of Job about human wisdom is that (1) there are important limits to the extent of our theoretical knowledge and understanding of God's purposes, (2) it is folly to judge God on the basis of our limited understanding, and (3) though God doesn't always explain or justify himself to us, he does give us crucial advice: practical wisdom consists in fearing him and avoiding evil. This last lesson is also the basic premise underlying the admonitions and exhortations contained in the book of Proverbs.

Proverbs is a collection of wise sayings of several kinds about various subjects and taken from sundry sources. What ties them together is an emphasis on *behavior*. Appropriate behavior is distinguished from inappropriate behavior, and the former is urged over the latter by observation, illustration, warning, and instruction. Attention is given to the *consequences* of behavior. Good behavior yields rewards, and bad behavior brings negative results. Thus Proverbs is primarily a work of *practical* wisdom. Some of this advice is prudential and some of it is moral. However, it is clear that morality is never sacrificed for expediency. Moreover, the overriding concern is to have a right relationship with God. Though the wisdom of Proverbs is based on experience and observation of nature and human society, it is also the case that the Lord gives wisdom (Prov. 2:6). The person who listens to wisdom "will be secure and will live at ease" (1:33 NRSV). Those who find wisdom will be happy (3:13), and wisdom is better than material things (3:14–15). Wisdom protects its possessor from immorality (chapter 7) and leads to physical and spiritual well-being (3:1–18). The only caution posed to the pursuer of wisdom is not to rely on one's own insight (3:5) but instead to begin one's search for wisdom by fearing God (9:10).

On this last point, the book of Job and the book of Proverbs are in agreement. However, one source of tension between the two works is that Proverbs appears to teach that the possession of practical wisdom assures its bearer of a good life, whereas Job makes it clear that righteous people can be the victims of undeserved affliction and misery. In the thirty-first chapter of Job, Job claims that his righteousness and piety are unsurpassed, and yet he is not rewarded for his goodness but instead divested of every earthly good but his own life. This tension between Job and Proverbs suggests the need to think carefully about wisdom and the good life. What exactly is the nature of the good life? Does true wisdom automatically lead to happiness? Is virtue its own reward? If not, what good is wisdom to someone who is overcome with misfortune? These questions, thrust upon every thoughtful reader of the Scriptures, were also topics of lively debate among classical Greek philosophers such as Plato and Aristotle. This issue is a common concern of those who seek wisdom from the Bible and those who turn to philosophy to find it. The Christian thinker will agree that true wisdom will lead to a life lived for God and that only such a life can be truly good. But this still leaves a number of questions unanswered. What is the role of wisdom in this life? To what extent can wisdom lead to temporal well-being for both individuals and societies? A general education can help Christians think through these and other important related questions by introducing them to the reflections of people who have attempted to answer them and by equipping them with the resources they need to find their own answers.

While the book of Job portrays the human search for justice and Proverbs offers guidance in the human quest for goodness, Ecclesiastes emphasizes the human pursuit of meaning and purpose. Is life really worth living? If so, what is the point of it all? These are questions that need to be answered by every person who seeks wisdom. The reader of Ecclesiastes will recognize both that these are the questions addressed by the "Teacher" (in Hebrew, *Qoheleth*) and that his answers to these questions are that everything is *meaningless*. Is this shocking claim the central lesson of this book of the Bible? There are good reasons for thinking it is not. We will follow Old Testament scholar Tremper Longman in finding the normative thesis of this work in the words of the "frame narrator," who both introduces and concludes the teaching of Qoheleth with remarks of his own as a "frame" around the comments of the latter. In the introduction (1:1–11), this editor merely summarizes the view of Qoheleth that everything is meaningless. In the editor's concluding remarks, after summarizing Qoheleth's main theme again (12:8), he affirms that Qoheleth was a professional "wise man" and teacher who conducted an honest search for the truth (12:9–10). However, his sayings have a painful sting like goads and nails (12:11). The editor warns his son about these sayings and also about the weariness caused by the incessant scholarship characterizing the pursuit of truth. He goes on to admonish his son to fear and obey God in order to be prepared for God's judgment. This orthodox editor seems to be warning his son not to follow those who pursue wisdom and truth without fearing and obeying God. He seems to be employing the teaching of Qoheleth as an example of a negative result of such godless reflection. True, Qoheleth does believe that God exists, but he shows his lack of piety in doubting the goodness and justice of God. Thus Qoheleth demonstrates his failure to conform to the admonition in Proverbs to "trust in the Lord with all your heart" and to "not rely on your own insight" (3:5 NRSV). This theme then ties the three biblical wisdom books together. The wise person is the one who fears, trusts, and obeys God rather than relying on his or her own understanding.

Wisdom in the Old Testament and Wisdom in Classical Greece

How does the Old Testament biblical perspective on wisdom compare with the classical Greek tradition? What they have in common is that both see wisdom as a valuable thing. They also agree that wisdom is essentially important *knowledge* and that wisdom has many forms. Though they refer to these forms using different language, both traditions feature the three kinds of wisdom discussed in the previous chapter: theoretical, practical, and productive.

Despite the lack of emphasis on theoretical wisdom in the three biblical "wisdom" books just discussed, the Old Testament nonetheless hints at the importance of understanding the world God made. For instance, the author of 1 Kings tells his readers that after Solomon became the king of Israel, he asked God for wisdom, and "God gave Solomon very great wisdom, discernment, and breadth of understanding as vast as the sand on the seashore" (4:29 NRSV). As a consequence, Solomon "would speak of trees, from the cedar that is in the Lebanon to the hyssop that grows in the wall," and "he would speak of animals, and birds, and reptiles, and fish" (v. 33 NRSV). Even if Solomon used this wisdom about nature as a basis for the practical advice contained in his proverbs, it is significant that his knowledge of the created world took the form of a classification of living things of the sort we find in the biological sciences today. And the author highlights the importance of Solomon's wisdom (including this theoretical wisdom about nature) by stressing that kings from all over the world who had heard about Solomon's wisdom sent representatives to his court to listen to him espouse it (v. 34).

The author of 1 Kings also informs us that God gave Solomon "discernment in administering justice" (3:11 NIV)—a skill Solomon employed when he settled a dispute between two women who each claimed to be an infant's mother (3:16–28). This valuable ability is an example of Solomon's *practical* wisdom, applied in this case to a matter of great moral significance. But Solomon is also reported to have exercised his practical wisdom in more prudential (and even sometimes ruthless) ways, demonstrated by his effectiveness in subduing his enemies (2:6 and 3:29), establishing himself as king (3:46), organizing his bureaucracy (4:1–19), and providing for his subjects (4:20–28). As we saw in the previous section of this chapter, Solomon's proverbs contain practical wisdom of both the moral and merely prudential kinds.

Solomon is also represented in 1 Kings as building both "the temple of the LORD" for God (6:1–38 NIV) and "the Palace of the Forest of Lebanon" for himself (7:1–12 NIV), as well as furnishings for the temple (7:13–51). Though Solomon's role in these construction projects was no doubt restricted to general oversight, the reader is given the impression that Solomon's wisdom was operative in the production of these buildings and their contents. As a matter of fact, it is more likely that those whom he enlisted to do the work for him had the productive wisdom to make these elaborate and beautiful edifices. This assignment of credit to Solomon's talented workers is justified by an explicit reference to one of them in 1 Kings 7:13–14: "King Solomon sent to Tyre and brought Huram . . . who was filled with wisdom, with understanding and with knowledge to do all kinds of bronze work" (NIV). The author of Exodus reports the LORD as saying something similar about Bezalel, whom the LORD chose to assist Moses in constructing the tabernacle: "See, I have chosen Bezalel, . . . and I have filled him with the Spirit of God, with wisdom, and understanding, with knowledge and with all kinds of skills—to make artistic designs for work in gold, silver, and bronze, to cut and set stones, to work in wood, and to engage in all kinds of crafts" (Exod. 31:1–5 NIV). So the Old Testament affirms the existence and value of productive wisdom as well as theoretical and practical wisdom—just as the ancient Greek tradition does.

Where these two traditions differ is in their view of the role of God in making a person wise. The Greeks believed wisdom could be acquired through sufficient experience, education, training, apprenticeship, and dialogue. On the other hand, the editors of the books of Job, Proverbs, and Ecclesiastes agree that people cannot be wise unless they fear the Lord. The theme that ties these three Old Testament wisdom books together is that there is no genuine wisdom apart from God. Human attempts to find wisdom without proper respect and reverence for God risk intellectual, moral, and spiritual error. These errors include arrogance, unrighteousness, and despair. We are, moreover, as the Bible reminds us, merely creatures, and there are important limits to the extent to which we can become wise. The Bible's affirmation of these limits can help explain why the Judeo-Christian tradition emphasizes practical wisdom over theoretical wisdom (and stresses theoretical wisdom less than the Greco-Roman tradition does). If we keep our creaturely limits in mind, we can pursue our Christian general learning in a way that gives glory to the Giver of wisdom.

Wisdom in the New Testament

When we turn to the New Testament, we find another wise man: Jesus. The gospels confirm his possession of this intellectual virtue. When the people in Jesus's hometown heard him teach, they were "amazed" at his wisdom and his miraculous powers (Matt. 13:54 NIV). Their astonishment about his wisdom could not have been due to Jesus's sudden acquisition of it, however, since according to Luke, as a child Jesus "grew and became strong," and "he was filled with wisdom" (2:40 NIV) and subsequently "grew in wisdom and in stature, and in favor with God and man" (2:52 NIV). Indeed, during his earthly ministry, Jesus exhibited his wisdom by what he did and said and by how he lived.

It does make sense that his neighbors were astounded at his ability to perform miracles. Whereas Solomon showed his wisdom about creation by being able to speak wisely about it, Jesus demonstrated his wisdom about nature by being able to exercise sovereign control over it. If we look only at the gospel of Mark, we read that Jesus calmed a storm (4:35–41), multiplied loaves and fishes to feed thousands of people (6:31–44 and 8:1–9), walked on the sea (6:48), and withered a fig tree (11:12). And these examples don't even include any of his healing miracles, which also demonstrate his knowledge of how to control specific aspects of the natural world. What all Jesus's "nature" miracles have in common is that they suggest his possession of theoretical wisdom about the universe. How could Jesus have known how to alter the course of nature unless he had a general knowledge of how the universe works?

Jesus's practical wisdom was manifested both by his teaching and by his example. As for the former, it is hard to find a finer example of moral insight than the content of Jesus's Sermon on the Mount (Matt. 5–7). Moreover, the crowds who heard his instruction "were amazed at his teaching, because he taught as one who had authority, and not as their teachers of the law" (7:28b–29 NIV). So Jesus distinguished himself not only as a *transmitter* of moral wisdom but also as a *source* of moral wisdom. And he practiced what he preached. When his opponents picked up stones to stone him, "Jesus said to them, 'I have shown you many good works from the Father. For which of these do you stone me?'" (John 10:32 NIV). His critics' response is telling: "We are not stoning you for any good work," they replied, "but for blasphemy, because you, a mere man, claim to be God" (10:33 NIV). They did not find fault with what Jesus *did* but rather with what Jesus *said* when he announced, "I and the Father are one" (10:30 NIV). Of course, some of them complained that he was demon-possessed (10:20), but others realized that a demon-possessed person couldn't teach or perform miracles as Jesus did (10:21). Finally, some accused him of being a "glutton and a drunkard" and faulted him for being "a friend of tax collectors and sinners," but Jesus responded by saying that "wisdom is proved right by her deeds" (Matt. 11:19 NIV). Jesus's lifestyle demonstrated the wisdom that his teaching expressed. In contrast to the false prophets against which he warns, Jesus is like a good tree that produces good fruit (Matt. 7:15–20).

Was Jesus productively wise? Did he know how to make beautiful and useful things? Well, he was both a carpenter's son (Matt. 13:55) and a carpenter (Mark 6:3). The word translated as "carpenter" here is the Greek word *tektōn*. It is related to the Greek word *techne*, which we saw in Chapter Five and which Aristotle used for the intellectual virtue we have been calling "productive wisdom." Recall that *techne* can be translated as "skill" or "art." A *tektōn* is an artisan or craftsperson skilled in the art of working with wood, stone, or metal. Since Jesus was most likely apprenticed to his father, he probably learned from his father how to make useful—and perhaps even beautiful—things made out of at least some of these materials. So, at least in terms of human ability, it is likely that Jesus was productively wise. But his miracles were due to his *super*human ability, and at least some of these works of wonder arguably manifest productive wisdom as well. Jesus's miracles of healing are good examples of miracles that exhibit productive wisdom. As we will see in Chapter Eleven, healing and carpentry (and stonemasonry, metalworking, etc.) are arts. These activities involve producing something worthwhile (a house, for example, in the latter case, and a healthy body in the former). It is plausible that Jesus's supernatural ability to heal people's bodies involved both theoretical wisdom about the workings of the human body and productive wisdom about how to make a sick or deformed body healthy or whole. And of course Jesus's desire to use these two forms of wisdom to promote human well-being is a consequence of his practical, moral wisdom and his love for human beings.

In sum, there is good reason to think that, like Solomon, Jesus was recognized for his theoretical, practical, and productive wisdom. But as Jesus said, "The Queen of the South . . . came from the ends of the earth to listen to Solomon's wisdom, and now something greater than Solomon is here" (Matt. 12:42 NIV). It is clear that by "something greater than Solomon," Jesus was referring to himself. So though Solomon was a wise man, Jesus is wiser. Indeed, Paul tells the church at Colossae that "in [Christ] are hidden all the treasures of wisdom and knowledge" (2:3 NIV). So Jesus Christ is both a very wise person and a source of great wisdom. After all, according to the prologue of John's gospel, Jesus is the Word of God, who "in the beginning . . . was God" (1:1) and who "gives light to [i.e., enlightens] everyone" (1:9) and who "became flesh and made his dwelling among us" (1:14 NIV). Jesus Christ is the Wisdom of God incarnate. As Paul told the Corinthians, Christ Jesus "has become for us wisdom from God" (1 Cor. 1:30 NIV).

The New Testament also affirms the importance of wisdom for those who follow Christ. In the parable of ten virgins, Jesus implicitly commends the five who wisely prepared for the coming of the bridegroom and condemns the five who foolishly did not (Matt. 25:1–13). He also assured his disciples that when they would be persecuted for following him, he would give them "words and wisdom" with which to respond to their accusers (Luke 21:15 NIV). Later, when the disciple Stephen experienced opposition from unbelieving fellow Hellenistic Jews, "they could not stand up against the wisdom the Spirit gave him as he spoke" (Acts 6:10 NIV). Additionally, the author of James exhorts those of his readers who lack wisdom to "ask God, who gives generously to all . . . and [wisdom] will be given to" them (1:5 NIV). Moreover, the same author encourages the "wise and understanding" to "show it by their good life, by deeds done in the humility that comes from wisdom" (3:13 NIV). And Paul tells the Colossians that he and Timothy "continually ask God to fill [them] with the knowledge of his will through all the wisdom and understanding that the Spirit gives, so that [they] may live a life worthy of the Lord and please him in every way" (1:9–10 NIV) and also that he and Timothy "proclaim [Christ], admonishing and teaching everyone with all wisdom, so that [Paul and Timothy] may present everyone fully mature in Christ" (1:28 NIV; see the similar verses in Eph. 1:17 and 5:15–17).

Clearly, the New Testament, like the Old Testament, presupposes and presents wisdom as a good thing. Jesus is wise. He wants his followers to be wise as well. He promises them that when they are persecuted for being his disciples, he will enable them to defend themselves wisely—which is precisely what happened when Stephen was challenged. Moreover, if we lack wisdom, we should ask God for it, and he will give it to us. When he does—by means of his Holy Spirit—we will be able to use our wisdom to grow in our knowledge of God and to be better able to live the way God wants us to live. Ultimately, our wisdom will contribute to our ability to become the kind of people God wants us to be: humble, loving, and mature in Christ.

A Note on Sources

For in-depth discussions of the three Old Testament wisdom books discussed in this chapter, see Tremper Longman's commentaries: *Job* (Grand Rapids: Baker Academic, 2012), *Proverbs* (Grand Rapids: Baker Academic, 2015), and *The Book of Ecclesiastes* (Grand Rapids: Eerdmans, 1997), in which Longman develops his "frame narrator" hypothesis. For a more general and theological introduction to these three Old Testament books, see *Old Testament Wisdom Literature: A Theological Introduction* (Downers Grove: InterVarsity Press Academic, 2011) by Craig G. Bartholomew and Ryan P. O'Dowd. Additional biblical context on the life of Solomon can be found in *The Expositor's Bible Commentary: 1 Samuel–2 Kings*, revised ed. (Grand Rapids: Zondervan, 2010), edited by Tremper Longman and David E. Garland. The New Testament books discussed in the third section of this chapter are Matthew, Mark, Luke, John, Acts, 1 Corinthians, Ephesians, Colossians, and James. Douglas Groothuis's book *Jesus* (Belmont: Wadsworth, 2003) is included in the Wadsworth Philosophers Series. This series "provides a brief and accessible insight into the ideas of major philosophers throughout history" (back cover). In this book, Groothuis characterizes Jesus as a philosopher (a lover of wisdom) and discusses Jesus's philosophical methods and views.

Questions for Reflection and Discussion

1. Based on your reading of Job, Proverbs, and Ecclesiastes, do you agree that the theme that ties them together is that the wise person is the one who fears, trusts, and obeys God rather than relying on his or her own understanding? Why or why not?

2. Can Christian general learners both follow the Bible in depending on God for wisdom and also follow the Greeks in finding wisdom through the exercise of natural human abilities? If so, how? If not, why not?

3. What are specific ways in which Christian general learners can both look to Jesus for a model of wisdom and make use of the wisdom God gives them in the course of their studies?

CHAPTER SEVEN

WISDOM IN THE ASIAN TRADITION

THE SEARCH FOR WISDOM IS NOT CONFINED TO THE NEAR EASTERN cultures that produced the Bible or to the Greco-Roman world that gave rise to European philosophy and science. Other major areas of the world that have wisdom traditions include Africa, India, and China. The cultivation and transmission of wisdom in all its forms is a universal human phenomenon. Aristotle said that human beings, by nature, desire to know. This desire has manifested itself in every human culture.

Learning from Other Wisdom Traditions

Humans at all times and in every place strive to discover the truth about ultimate reality, the meaning of human life, the character of human goodness, the nature of right behavior, and the essence of beauty. Cultural myths, religious creeds, and philosophical theories are all human attempts to make sense of life and the world. They reflect the human desire to know the truth about reality and to understand the meaning of life. In a Christian general education, this search manifests itself in learning for the sake of theoretical wisdom. The universal thoughtful human quest to live well has resulted in cultural oral and written collections of proverbs, riddles, parables, and maxims of various kinds. Religious and ethical codes also embody behavioral guidance, and normative theories in philosophical ethics investigate the nature of goodness and rightness. Ideally, Christian general learning includes aspects aimed at moral reflection, character development, and education for responsible action. This is learning for practical wisdom. Human cultures also contain a variety of arts and techniques. Human creativity finds religious expression in cult, ritual, and worship. Throughout the history of a human group, a growing body of technical lore accompanies the manufacture of tools and the production of artworks. Today we see the proliferation of this lore in a plethora of "how to" books (though many of these fall into the category of practical wisdom). Training in specific technologies is the domain of engineering and trades of various kinds. However, *general* productive wisdom is appropriately included in a Christian general education. The cultivation of theoretical, practical, and productive wisdom in the quest for truth, goodness, and beauty is universal. The Christian general learner should seek these forms of wisdom wherever they can be found.

This universal human search for wisdom means that Christian general learning ought to extend beyond Europe and the Near East. The Greco-Roman and Judeo-Christian traditions are not the only repositories of truth, goodness, and beauty. Western Christians can learn a lot from the rest of the world. To put this point another way, there is a sense in which Christian general learning ought to be *multicultural* (though as indicated in Chapter Five, this does not mean that such learning must adhere to multicultural*ism*—at least of the radical postmodern variety). In order for Christian general educational programs in Europe and North America to benefit from the wisdom of other cultures (as they already have from the wisdom of the Greco-Roman and Judeo-Christian cultural traditions), Christian general learners in these contexts must engage in a study of other cultures from the standpoint of their own culture and the revelation of God in the Bible. When they do so, they ought to follow the advice of St. Augustine, who likened the Christian employment of wisdom from non-Christian sources to the ancient Israelites' appropriation of Egyptian gold and silver when they were fleeing from Pharaoh under the leadership of Moses. Though non-Christian traditions will inevitably include falsehoods that Christians ought to reject (analogous to the Egyptian idols that it was best for the Israelites to leave behind), these traditions may well also contain truths that Christians ought to accept. The Christian doctrines of general revelation and of common grace, according to which God reveals aspects of himself and his will in creation and graciously provides many good things to all human beings in common, provide a theological basis for the expectation that truth, goodness, and beauty can be found outside the Judeo-Christian context.

How should Christian general learners who live in cultures formed and informed by the Bible and European ideas and ideals look for wisdom elsewhere? How can the precious intellectual, moral, and aesthetic "gold" they discover in other cultural contexts supplement and even correct what they treasure at home? So far, we have found that wisdom is knowledge of important matters. It is knowledge that involves the heart as well as the mind. Whereas the mind grasps particular truths, the heart discerns which of these truths are most worth knowing. From Aristotle, we learned that there are three general kinds of wisdom corresponding to the three categories of truth, goodness, and beauty. When we turned to the Scriptures, we found that the overriding theme is that genuine wisdom is based on a proper attitude toward God and toward oneself: wise people fear God and do not place excessive confidence in their own understanding. A lot more could be said about wisdom in the classical Western and biblical traditions. Not enough has been said about either of these traditions, nor will enough be said in this chapter about wisdom in the Asian wisdom traditions for the purpose of an adequate evaluation of the latter in light of the former. However, we do have sufficient grounds to offer some general principles that can be gleaned from the Judeo-Christian tradition and to make some tentative evaluative claims on the basis of them for illustrative purposes.

First, Christians should evaluate every wisdom claim from the standpoint of the Scriptures. This applies just as much to Greek and Roman ideas about wisdom as to non-Western notions, such as those contained in the Asian wisdom traditions we will examine in the next two sections of this chapter (Confucianism and Buddhism). This first general principle is that we should test every human attempt to find wisdom from the standpoint of God's special revelation in the Bible. If something we encounter is clearly inconsistent with our best understanding of Scripture, it should be rejected. This is *the principle of the primacy of Scripture.* Second, our understanding of a given tradition's views about wisdom is always a matter of a certain amount of interpretation on our part. This principle applies not only to our understanding of wisdom in non-Western thought and how we construe Greco-Roman thinking but also to our understanding of the Bible itself. This is *the principle of the necessity of interpretation.* Third, before we evaluate a foreign truth claim, character trait recommendation, behavioral policy proposal, or aesthetic judgment, we need to make sure that we have taken steps to achieve an adequate understanding of it and of any reasons offered in support of it. This is *the principle of the importance of understanding.* Fourth, these first three principles leave open the possibility that we could learn something from other traditions. This learning could either take the form of a supplementation of our existing thought about wisdom or even a basis for amending what we think about it. That is, what we learn from non-Christian, non-Western traditions might either extend or correct what we already believe and/or value. A revision of our beliefs and/or values would be warranted under such circumstances if we became convinced that the new perspective was generally consistent with the Scriptures and that our previous interpretation of the Bible was subject to reasonable doubt. This is *the principle of the virtue of openness to correction.* Finally, when we have been as charitable as we can be in our attempt to adequately understand and fairly evaluate the contents of a particular wisdom tradition, we should be willing to reject anything that is clearly inconsistent with what we know to be true, good, and beautiful. This is *the principle of the virtue of consistency*. Applying these principles in the evaluation of a wisdom claim requires a mixture of the attitudes of confidence and humility. This process requires a critical openness to all human intellectual traditions from the standpoint of Christian faith.

Learning from the Confucian Wisdom Tradition

Our first experiment in cross-cultural intellectual investigation will involve consideration of a prominent philosophical approach of ancient China. This is the philosophy of Confucianism. The founder of this philosophy, Confucius (or "K'ung Fu-tzu"—Master K'ung), was an ancient Chinese teacher whom scholars believe lived from 551 to 479 BCE. Some of his disciples (or disciples of his disciples) recorded some of his teachings, and these lessons have been preserved in the "analects" (sayings) of Confucius. Confucian scholars continued to discuss *The Analects* after Confucius died, and his thought subsequently had a profound impact on Chinese culture and history. The Confucian philosophical tradition has been modified in various ways over the centuries, but its general contours have remained fundamentally unchanged, and its influence can still be discerned in China and some other East and Southeast Asian cultures today. Our brief and general survey of Confucianism will focus only on *The Analects* and so will not include later developments of Confucius's ideas.

Before we look carefully at the main elements of Confucius's thought, we need to discuss a potential obstacle that could prevent us from adequately understanding, sufficiently appreciating, and fairly assessing both Confucius and his philosophy. This obstacle involves our general tendency as human beings to stereotype what is foreign, alien, exotic, or unfamiliar to us and our specific tendency as Westerners to stereotype anything non-Western. A stereotype is a widely held but overly simplified and often distorted way of thinking about someone or something. Western stereotypes of Asian people and cultures can tend either to portray them in an overly negative way (e.g., to vilify them) or to represent them in an overly positive way (e.g., to romanticize them). Neither of these tendencies is conducive to discovering the truth about them or to treating them with sufficient respect.

A stereotypical image often associated with Confucius is that of a wizened and doddering old man sporting a long beard and wearing a floor-length robe. The stereotype also portrays Confucius as someone whose only utterances are isolated and pithy pronouncements on the human condition. This stereotype has led to a rash of "Confucian sayings" that at first appear to be sage pieces of advice but in the second half of the sentence are revealed to be the setup for a pun. Among the many examples that can be found on the Internet is the following: "Confucius says, 'Man who make mistake in elevator wrong on many levels.'" Though these jokes may be funny, they can also tend to perpetuate stereotypes of Confucius and of Chinese people and Asians more generally (note the broken English of the example). We should strive to avoid these stereotypes in our search for truth, goodness, and beauty in Asian wisdom traditions.

What gives stereotypes their power is that they are based on truth. Confucius's teaching really is encapsulated in relatively concise statements. But these brief sayings are meant to stimulate deep thinking about matters of fundamental importance to human life rather than to elicit laughter about matters of superficial and trivial interest to human beings. And what Confucius considered to be of paramount importance was (1) *education for wisdom and virtue* by means of (2) *master–apprentice communal learning* involving (3) *dialogue, demonstration, and ritual* for the sake of (4) *active and harmonious political engagement*. Above all else, Confucius valued the cultivation of intellectual and moral virtue (competence and character) through a process of discipleship that involved both expanding the mind and directing the heart for the purpose of good citizenship.

First, the proximate goal of Confucian education is the formation of a "gentleman" (Chinese: *junzi*). Confucius used this word only for the *intellectually and morally* elite rather than for the *socially and aristocratically* elite. That is, he applied it to people with a *good intellect and character* rather than to those with a *good origin and pedigree.* Consequently, in his view, gentlemen are *made* and not *born*. Confucius contrasts gentlemen with "small" men and "vulgar" men.

> "A gentleman considers what is just; a small man considers what is expedient."—Analect 4.16

> "A gentleman is easygoing and free; a vulgar man is always tense and fretful."—Analect 7.37

The supreme virtue of a gentleman is "humanity" ("goodness," "virtue," or "benevolence"—Chinese: *ren*). For this reason, Confucius thinks of the education of a gentleman as involving primarily the cultivation of humanity (the same expression we borrowed from Seneca in Chapter Two to characterize the common goal of general learning shared by the orators and the philosophers in the Greco-Roman tradition). And the cultivation of humanity yields *general* intellectual and moral improvement rather than *specific* technical and vocational development. Confucius captures this aim of education (which we affirmed in Chapter Two to be characteristic of general learning) with a metaphorical aphorism: "A gentleman is not a pot" (2.12). That is, a generally educated person is not limited in capacity or restricted in usefulness but instead able to exercise a breadth of skills for a diversity of purposes. Similarly, "the Master said, 'The gentleman considers the whole rather than the parts. The small man considers the parts rather than the whole'" (2.14).

Second, Confucius related to his students as a master to his apprentices or disciples. As a result, he followed the "sage on the stage" pedagogical model—at least to some extent. That is, he viewed himself as a person with enough wisdom and virtue to be able to provide answers to some of the questions his students asked him and to model some of the attitudes and behaviors he expected them to emulate. In this respect, he was unlike Socrates, whom we characterized above as a person in pursuit of wisdom (a philosopher) rather than a person in possession of wisdom (a sage). But Confucius also practiced the "guide on the side" pedagogical approach by asking questions his students were responsible to answer for themselves: "The Master said, 'I enlighten only the enthusiastic; I guide only the fervent. After I have lifted up one corner of a question, if the student cannot discover the other three, I do not repeat'" (7.8). It seems clear that Confucius wanted his students both to learn important truths from him and also to learn how to think for themselves. However, he had no patience for intellectual conversations engaged in merely for their own sake: "The Master said, 'I cannot abide these people who are capable of spending a whole day together in a display of wits without ever hitting upon a single truth'" (15.7). Even so, he was sensitive to his students' different learning needs and adopted strategies suitable to their personalities: "The Master said, 'Ran Qui is slow, therefore I push him; Zilu has energy for two, therefore I hold him back'" (11.22).

Third, Confucius taught his students by means of precept, example, and ritual. As for precept, Confucius relied on traditional wisdom conveyed by books such as the *Changes*, the *Poems*, and the *Documents* (see Analects 7.17 and 7.18). In doing so, he showed himself to be "conservative" rather than "progressive": "The Master said, 'I transmit, I invent nothing. I trust and love the past'" (7.1). But Confucius was just as much opposed to a blind reception of tradition as he was against a complete disregard of ancient wisdom: "The Master said, 'To study without thinking is futile. To think without studying is dangerous'" (2.15). Confucius also emphasized the importance of modeling good attitudes and behaviors for others. When he said, "Shun was certainly one of those who knew how to govern by inactivity. . . . He sat reverently on the throne, facing south—and that was all" (15.5), he meant that Shun was leading his people solely by the power of his moral example. Confucius also commented on how easy it is to learn from others just by observing them: "The Master said, 'Put me in the company of any two people at random—they will invariably have something to teach me. I can take their qualities as a model and their defects as a warning'" (7.22). Finally, Confucius believed that ritual is an essential means of learning how to behave properly: "The Master said, 'A gentleman enlarges his learning through literature and restrains himself with ritual; therefore, he is not likely to go wrong'" (6.27). He believed that rituals, practiced in ceremonies, taught people to be governed by an inward principle of propriety (Chinese: *li*) rather than by externally imposed laws. But there must be a balance between moral goodness (*ren*) and ritual propriety (*li*): "The Master said, 'Authority without generosity, ceremony without reverence, mourning without grief—these, I cannot bear to contemplate'" (3.26).

Finally, the ultimate goal of Confucian education is the cultivation of good citizens and leaders. Consequently, Confucius's approach to education was less like that of the Greco-Roman philosophers and more like that of the orators from that tradition, who valued a general education primarily for its contribution to the development of a moral character and to preparation for good citizenship and political well-being. One of Confucius's disciples put this orientation starkly: "Zixia said, 'Leisure from politics should be devoted to learning. Leisure from learning should be devoted to politics'" (19.13). But one should never cease from loving to learn, since this attitude is essential for the maintenance of intellectual and moral virtue (see 17.8). For Confucius, however, such ongoing enthusiastic learning would need to have a primarily practical moral and political purpose. As his student Zigong said, "Our Master's views on culture can be gathered, but it is not possible to hear his views on the nature of things and the Way of Heaven" (5.13). But we should not conclude from this observation that Confucius valued only practical and productive but not theoretical wisdom. Instead, it seems clear that his silences about transcendent and ultimate things implied a respect for realities that he considered to be too sacred to discuss. Indeed, his brief autobiography demonstrates his belief in a higher moral order: "The Master said, 'At fifteen, I set my mind upon learning. At thirty, I took my stand. At forty, I had no doubts. At fifty, I knew the will of Heaven. At sixty, my ear was attuned. At seventy, I follow all the desires of my heart without breaking any rule'" (2.4). Though we may question the intellectual and moral perfection implied by this summary, there is plenty in the life and teaching of Confucius to provide Christian students with intellectual, moral, and aesthetic "gold" to supplement the Judeo-Christian and Greco-Roman riches they already have.

How should we evaluate Confucianism on the basis of the five principles introduced in the previous section of this chapter? We have already seen that a Confucian approach to education is similar in some important respects to aspects of the Greco-Roman liberal arts tradition. Like the latter tradition, Confucianism values the general cultivation of intellectual and moral virtues. This Chinese tradition also shares with the oratorical liberal arts tradition an emphasis on education for the sake of good citizenship. In virtue of this common focus, these two traditions stress practical wisdom over theoretical wisdom—as the biblical tradition does but the philosophical approach to the liberal arts does not. Moreover, both Confucius and Jesus adopted the master-disciple model and both made use of instruction, example, and practice as methods of teaching. That is, both provided their apprentices with opportunities to acquire propositional knowledge of important truths, recognitional knowledge of appropriate behavior, and procedural knowledge of useful skills. So, assuming we have interpreted and understood Confucius's analects adequately, there is much in Confucianism to affirm from the standpoint of both the Greco-Roman and biblical (Judeo-Christian) traditions. And it is reasonable to think that many Christians—especially those who live in cultural contexts that downplay tradition—could learn from Confucius's teaching about ritual as a means of developing an interior sense of the kind of outward behavior that demonstrates appropriate respect for others.

So Christians can find much to commend in Confucianism. But from a biblical standpoint, this Chinese philosophy is also incomplete in certain important respects (as are the Greco-Roman philosophies). These omissions are due in part to Confucius's reticence to speak about "the Way of Heaven." They are also a result of his not having had access to God's special revelation in the Bible. In the first place, though Confucius recognized the existence of human ignorance, vice, and immorality, he did not have a doctrine of *sin*, according to which the fundamental human problem is a stubborn and prideful condition of rebellion against God that humans are incapable of altering without God's help. As a result, Confucius (like Aristotle) was overly optimistic about the sufficiency of human effort alone to produce the intellectual and moral transformation he encouraged his students to achieve. Second, though there is much to be admired in the sort of learning community Confucius developed, his failure to speak about the Way of Heaven meant that he was unable to encourage his students to turn to and depend on the divine Teacher for wisdom. Consequently, the school of Confucius (like the school of Athens) was hampered by its consisting only in "horizontal" human relationships (rather than in both horizontal and "vertical" divine–human relationships). Third, without being guided by God's Word and enlightened and empowered by the Holy Spirit, students who are seeking to grow in wisdom will not be able to benefit fully from a human teacher's instruction, example, and assigned exercises. Finally, though both Greco-Roman and Asian philosophies and pedagogies can help equip us to be good citizens in the earthly societies in which we live, we need God's Word and Spirit to enable us to become good citizens in the heavenly Kingdom of God. Of course, this observation applies to any merely human wisdom tradition—including the other Asian philosophy we will discuss now: Buddhism.

Learning from the Buddhist Wisdom Tradition

Our second experiment in cross-cultural intellectual investigation involves a wisdom tradition that originated just north of India near the foothills of the Himalayan Mountain Range in modern-day Nepal.

The founder of this tradition is usually called the Buddha, but his personal name in Sanskrit (the classical language of India) was Siddhartha Gautama. "Buddha" is an honorific title that means, "Awakened [or "Enlightened"] One." Recent research suggests that the Buddha lived from around 490 to 410 BCE.

Scholars generally agree on the following chronology of the Buddha's life: He was born into an aristocratic family. He married at sixteen. At twenty-nine, soon after the birth of his son, he left home in pursuit of religious knowledge. After considering himself to have attained enlightenment at the age of thirty-five, he spent the rest of his life engaged in religious teaching until he died at eighty.

Buddhist legends fill in the gaps with stories about the events in the Buddha's life that are regarded as having the most religious significance. According to traditional Buddhist sources, he grew up in his father's palaces, where he lived a life of luxury. Before leaving his wife and child, he made four visits outside the palaces in a chariot. During each of these trips, he witnessed a different sign. On the first visit, he saw an old man. On the second, he observed a sick man. And on the third, he encountered a corpse being carried to the cremation ground. These three experiences had a profound effect on him and convinced him that human life—even within the relative comfort and security of his father's palaces—is transient and characterized by suffering in the form of aging, illness, and death. On his fourth visit outside the palaces, he came across a religious beggar and was inspired by this man's example to depart his family and home in search of religious insight as a homeless mendicant.

After he renounced his privileged and complacent former existence, the Buddha sought assistance from first one teacher and then another. Both taught him meditational techniques that enabled him to attain serene, blissful, and even sublime states of consciousness, which he valued. However, he eventually moved on from them unsatisfied, because their techniques left the problem of suffering unresolved when he returned to his ordinary state of consciousness. Subsequently, the

Buddha decided to try his own techniques, which involved extreme austerities for the purpose of subduing his appetites and passions. These methods included holding his breath for longer and longer periods of time and severely reducing his consumption of food until he ate only a tiny morsel a day. As a result of these deprivations, the Buddha experienced physical pain, weakness, and disability rather than an alleviation of his suffering. He concluded that neither the extreme of self-indulgence nor the extreme of self-mortification were effective means to this end. He chose instead a "middle way" between these extremes.

According to Buddhist tradition, after following this middle way for a while, the Buddha progressed rapidly, until one night, under what has come to be known as a "bodhi" tree, he achieved his goal of complete awakening or enlightenment (which is what "bodhi" means). Throughout that night, and by means of his matured practice of meditation, he had a succession of three insights, each corresponding to a major component of Buddhist thought. First, he was able to remember each of his past lives in full detail. This provided him with insight into his own experience of *samsara* (reincarnation), the ongoing cycle of birth, death, and rebirth. Second, he was able to see how the birth, death, and rebirth of all kinds of beings in the universe were a result of their good and bad deeds. This gave him insight into *karma*, the natural law of justice that determines the conditions of an individual's rebirth on the basis of the degree of their merit or demerit. And third, he came to know that, due to the elimination of his spiritual impurities, he was no longer subject to either craving or ignorance and, as a result, was released from the cycle of rebirth (samsara based on karma). This liberation from desire, delusion, and endless rebirth is called *nirvana* (which means "extinguishing"). In nirvana, the Buddha found what he had been seeking: the cessation of both suffering and rebirth.

Following his awakening/enlightenment (when he officially became a Buddha), the Buddha decided to communicate the knowledge he had acquired in the form of what has come to be known as the *dharma* ("teachings"). The essence of the dharma is contained in his first sermon, which is entitled *Setting in Motion the Wheel of the Dharma*. The substance of this sermon is the Four Noble Truths. The first noble truth is that life is characterized by suffering. This is the insight the Buddha had when he ventured forth from his father's palaces and saw the aging, the sick, and the dead. But suffering also includes any dissatisfaction or discontent as well. The second noble truth is that the cause of suffering is craving (or attachment). The third noble truth is that suffering can be eliminated by the cessation of craving (or attachment). The fourth noble truth is that one can extinguish his or her cravings and attachments by means of following the Eightfold Path (which will be described in the next paragraph). Notice that the four noble truths can be articulated using a medical analogy: suffering is the disease, craving is the cause, the elimination of craving is the cure, and following the Eightfold Path is the treatment that leads to the cure.

The Eightfold Path is also known as the "middle way" because it is meant to lead those who follow it on a course that lies between an indulgent life and a deprived life (the route of moderation that the Buddha chose just before his awakening/enlightenment). The "eight" of the Eightfold Path are eight specific "ways" a Buddhist employs, on an ongoing basis, to facilitate the elimination of suffering and the cultivation of flourishing. These eight ways are divided into the three categories of wisdom, morality, and meditation:

Wisdom: (1) right understanding and (2) right resolve;
Morality: (3) right speech, (4) right action, and (5) right livelihood; and
Meditation: (6) right effort, (7) right mindfulness, and (8) right meditation.

The Eightfold Path provides Buddhists with a means of self-transformation aimed at the goal of becoming like the Buddha. Meditation provides the means, through the elimination of ignorance and selfish desire (and therefore suffering), to the attainment of the goals of wisdom and virtue.

The three categories of the Eightfold Path (wisdom, morality, and meditation) can be seen as corresponding, at least roughly, to the three types of wisdom we have been discussing in this book: theoretical, practical, and productive. Recall that theoretical wisdom is wisdom about what is true, practical wisdom is wisdom about how to live a good life, and productive wisdom is wisdom about how to make beautiful and/or useful things. We can understand the Buddhist wisdom category as aimed in large part at the acquisition of theoretical wisdom, the Buddhist morality category as targeting mostly the attainment of practical wisdom and moral virtue, and the Buddhist meditation category as meant to facilitate the achievement of a kind of productive wisdom.

The wisdom category contains right understanding (or right view), which involves accepting the Buddhist teachings and confirming them on the basis of one's personal experience. Fundamentally, these teachings include the Four Noble Truths. But they also entail the doctrines of impermanence and *anatta* ("no-self"). The doctrine of impermanence is that there is nothing in reality that persists unchanged across time. And if there is *nothing* that persists unchanged through time, then there is no *self* that persists unchanged through time. So the doctrine of impermanence entails the doctrine of anatta. The Buddha believed that knowledge of these doctrines would help one cultivate right resolve (being committed to cultivating right attitudes). Knowing that there is nothing permanent and unchanging can enable one to see not only why life is suffering (the first noble truth) but also why being attached to something causes suffering (the second noble truth). Our desires to hold onto things we consider good (such as youth, health, and life) presuppose that those things will last, and so it is no wonder that if nothing lasts, those desires will inevitably be frustrated, and we will suffer as a result (in the form of disappointment, discouragement, dissatisfaction, etc.). On the assumption that frustrated desire is the only cause of suffering, it makes sense that refraining from craving or attachment altogether would lead to the cessation of suffering (the third noble truth). The Buddha believed that knowledge of this truth can help someone resolve to do what it takes to stop craving things and wanting to hold onto them.

How can one live well in a world in which one knows that nothing—not even oneself—has an essential nature to give it enough permanence to make it a source of satisfaction for one's desires? The Buddhist answer to this question, as we have seen, is that one must learn to stop craving things in such a way as to be attached to them. That is, one must eliminate one's *selfish* desires—those desires that make one grasping, greedy, and willing to harm others for the sake of self-satisfaction. And what one needs for this purpose, according to the Buddha, is the practical wisdom that consists in knowing how to be moral, how to be virtuous. And this wisdom consists at least in knowing how to practice right speech (speaking truthfully, thoughtfully, and sensitively), right action (abstaining from such wrong actions as killing, stealing, and inappropriate sensuality), and right livelihood (refraining from making a living in a way that causes harm to others). Notice that these practices combine selfless benevolence to others (which, along with understanding and nonattachment, is a cardinal Buddhist virtue) and the avoidance of harm to others (which is the principle of *ahimsa*, the most fundamental principle of Buddhist ethics).

In the Buddhist wisdom tradition, one also needs to be productively wise. One needs to know how to make oneself into a virtuous person, how to cultivate a Buddha-like character. That is, one needs to know how to acquire a character that would be both attractive for its own sake (i.e., beautiful) and conducive to the compassionate cultivation of wisdom (understanding), moral virtue (benevolence), and meditation (nonattachment) in oneself and others (i.e., useful and beneficial). So for Buddhists, knowing how to live well (practical wisdom) is closely tied to knowing how to make oneself into someone capable of living well (productive wisdom).

The category of meditation in the Eightfold Path provides the techniques considered by Buddhists to be necessary and sufficient for the attainment of this productive wisdom. Recall that this category includes right effort (controlling one's thoughts in such a way as to produce positive states of mind), right mindfulness (cultivating an ability to sustain a full and focused awareness), and right meditation (developing deep levels of mental calm by concentrating one's mind and integrating one's personality). The ultimate goal of meditation (considered to be a combination of these three practices) is to bring about a state of mind that can be "likened to purified gold in the malleable and pliable state from which precious objects are formed by a skilled artisan. In this case, the artisan is the meditator who, having access to the deep levels of the psyche, is equipped to undertake the task of remodeling himself" (Keown, 91). So a meditator's productive wisdom is wisdom about how to make oneself into a beautiful and beneficial person.

According to this analysis, the Buddhist wisdom tradition is like the Judeo-Christian, Greco-Roman, and Confucian traditions in offering what it considers to be wisdom of all three kinds: theoretical, practical, and productive. This tradition proposes a view of reality, a moral ideal, and a strategy for attaining that ideal on the basis of that view by means of a set of time-tested techniques. What can the Christian general learner glean from this wisdom tradition, if anything? It is now time to employ our five general principles for the Judeo-Christian evaluation of other wisdom traditions in order to answer that question.

The twentieth-century Roman Catholic monk Thomas Merton believed that Christians could learn from Buddhism in spite of important differences between these traditions. Merton's friend, the Vietnamese Buddhist monk Thich Nhat Hanh, goes further. His view is that the two traditions are consistent with each other and, even more, merely different expressions of the same fundamental view of reality and the same ideal for human flourishing. In his view, Buddhists and Christians are merely using different language to express the same ideas (or different ideas that provide alternative means to engage in the same way of life—which for him is the only thing that truly matters). Christian students can employ the five principles to show that Merton's approach is superior to Nhat Hanh's. A proper understanding of the two traditions, based on reasonable interpretations of both the Buddhist dharma and the Bible, supports the view that they are fundamentally inconsistent in important respects. But such an understanding will also reveal significant commonalities.

According to the Bible, God's creation may be temporary, but God is eternal: "[The heavens and the earth] will perish but [the Lord] will endure" (Ps. 102:26 NRSV). Moreover, though we humans are mortal, we will persist throughout this life and after death as the same selves God created, not to be reborn into another earthly life, but to be raised from the dead, judged by God, and saved by Christ (if we trust in him): "And just as it is appointed for mortals to die once, and after that the judgment, so Christ, having been offered once to bear the sins of many, will appear a second time, not to deal with sin, but to save those who are eagerly waiting for him" (Heb. 9:27–28 NRSV). So the Buddhist doctrines of impermanence, no-self (anatta), and reincarnation (samsara) contradict the teaching of the Christian scriptures. Also, these theoretical differences entail practical ones. The Buddhist doctrines of impermanence and anatta rule out the possibility of divine assistance in the process of becoming wise and virtuous. At its core, Buddhism is essentially a philosophy of self-improvement. But according to the Christian gospel, God saves human beings from the penalty and power of sin through the incarnation, death, resurrection, and ascension of God the Son, Jesus Christ, and through the sanctifying work of the Holy Spirit, a real divine person. In addition, God's saving work through the Son and the Spirit involves both mercy (forgiveness of sin) and grace (power for virtue). So the Buddhist doctrines of karma (you reap what you sow) and nirvana (liberation from ignorance and suffering by means of meditation alone) are inconsistent with biblical teaching.

In spite of these important differences, there are also meaningful agreements—agreements that can serve as bases for Christians to learn from Buddhists. These agreements can be found in all three wisdom categories. Christians and Buddhists agree on the theory that every human life involves suffering, that at least much of this suffering is a result of selfish desire, that at least some suffering can therefore be alleviated or eradicated by the elimination of selfish desire, and that it is possible for people to succeed in eliminating these desires. Moreover, both traditions affirm the moral ideals of nonviolence and benevolence, not only as they are manifested behaviorally, but also as they are rooted in virtuous character traits such as compassion and selflessness. Finally, both Buddhists and Christians can affirm meditation as at least one means that can be employed for the cultivation of wisdom and virtue (and Christians can benefit from a study of Buddhist meditation). Of course, Christians will also say that some suffering can be redemptive (Rom. 5:3–5), that God assists us in our moral and spiritual transformation (Phil. 2:12–13), and that human flourishing requires meditation on God's word (Ps. 1:2–3). And Christians will point out that, whereas Buddhism is based on human wisdom, the source of Christianity is divine wisdom.

A Note on Sources

Augustine's comparison of the Israelites' plundering of Egyptian gold and silver with the Christian appropriation of non-Christian wisdom occurs in *De Doctrina Christiana* (*On Christian Doctrine*), chapter 40, paragraph 60. A good edition of Confucius's *Analects* is *The Analects of Confucius*, translation and notes by Simon Leys (New York: Norton, 1997). For an additional Christian perspective on Confucius and Confucianism, see Gregg Ten Elshof's *Confucius for Christians: What an Ancient Chinese Worldview Can Teach Us about Life in Christ* (Grand Rapids: Eerdmans, 2015). The first part of the Buddhism chapter relies heavily on Damien Keown's *Buddhism: A Very Short Introduction* (Oxford: Oxford University Press, 1996). The Buddha's teaching is preserved in the Pali Canon (a collection of Buddhist scripture written in the ancient Pali language). Thomas Merton's final views on the relationship between Christianity and Buddhism can be found in his *The Asian Journal of Thomas Merton* (New York: New Directions Books, 1975), edited by Patrick Hart, James Laughlin, and Naomi Burton Stone, which was published posthumously. And Thich Nhat Hanh's attempt to harmonize Buddhism and Christianity is contained in his *Living Buddha, Living Christ* (New York: Riverhead Books, 1995).

Questions for Reflection and Discussion

1. Do you agree that Christians can learn about truth, goodness, and beauty from non-Christian and non-Western wisdom traditions? If so, why? If not, why not?

2. Do you find anything in the teaching of Confucius that you believe is worthy of acceptance or anything in the example of Confucius that you think merits your emulation? If so, what are these claims, attitudes, and/or behaviors? If not, why not?

3. What is your view about the relationship between Buddhism and Christianity? Do you think they are completely incompatible, compatible in some respects but not in others, or completely compatible? Why?

CHAPTER EIGHT

HUMAN WISDOM AND DIVINE WISDOM

IN CHAPTER FOUR, OUR INITIAL FOCUS WAS ON THE TENSION between the critical questioning model of Socrates of Athens and the confident commitment called for by Jesus of Jerusalem. Our recommendation was to strive to reconcile the Socratic philosophical way of life with the way of Christian discipleship by adopting the Augustinian motto of "faith seeking understanding." We illustrated how Christians could engage in this Augustinian intellectual practice today by drawing on the resources of philosophy, science, biblical hermeneutics, and theology to come to their own reasoned view about the resolution of the creation–evolution debate. In doing so, they can be responsible citizens of both Jerusalem and Athens by balancing their Christian commitment with an openness to revising their views about the relationship between science and Scripture. And as a result, they can hope—with God's help—to grow in both confidence and courage.

In this chapter, we will think about a similar tension between Jerusalem and Athens that tends to turn some believers into Tertullians (Christians who reject nonbiblical sources of wisdom). This is the tension between human wisdom and divine wisdom. General learners achieve human wisdom on the basis of natural reason. Christian disciples receive divine wisdom on the basis of supernatural faith. A Christian general education would ideally result in comprehensive wisdom resulting from both of these sources. But some statements and admonitions St. Paul of Jerusalem included in some of his epistles seem to imply that Christians should avoid human wisdom and limit themselves to divine wisdom. We find this apparent Pauline opinion in 1 Corinthians and in his letter to the church at Colossae.

St. Paul on Human Wisdom and Divine Wisdom

Consider first Paul's first letter to the church at Corinth, where we find his criticism of wisdom—that is, *human* wisdom. Here there is a sharp contrast between the "wisdom of the world" (1:20) and the "wisdom of God" (1:21 NIV). Paul's rejection of the former in favor of the latter poses a challenge to the Christian defender of general learning. Is the wisdom produced by general Christian education always and in every way conducive to Christian ends? This question must be considered carefully in light of Paul's remarks to the church at Corinth.

Paul's discussion of wisdom in his first letter to the Corinthians occurs primarily in the first four chapters of this epistle. Evidently, oratorical skill and logical acumen were present and highly prized in the Corinthian church. Paul is thankful that they were "enriched" in Christ "with all kinds of *speech* and with all *knowledge*" (1:5 NIV—emphasis mine). However, he had preached the gospel to them *without wisdom and eloquence,* "lest the cross of Christ be emptied of its power" (1:17 NIV). That is, Paul's evangelistic strategy was to rely on the *substance* of the gospel message rather than on a skillful oratorical *style*. From a purely human standpoint, this is a foolish method of persuasion. The idea that the salvation of humankind should be accomplished by means of a man dying like a criminal on a cross seems ridiculous. Shouldn't Christians employ the best thinking and speaking skills in their attempts to win converts to a life based on this initially implausible and offensive claim?

We can glean a fourfold reply to this question in Paul's comments to the Corinthians. First, skilled rhetoric and logic are not *necessary* to communicate the gospel effectively. The best argument for this is the example of Paul himself, who brought many to Christ, in spite of the fact that "[his] message and [his] preaching were not with wise and persuasive words" (2:4 NIV). Second, human wisdom is not *sufficient* to bring people to a saving knowledge of God. Paul says, "The world did not know God through wisdom" (1:21 NRSV). This failure of the world to know God through wisdom is partially because the message of a crucified Christ is folly from a human perspective (1:23). Third, he implies that the unadorned "word of the cross" is more effective without oratorical flourish than with it. Indeed, this is why he "did not come with eloquence or human wisdom as [he] proclaimed to [the Corinthians] the testimony about God" (2:1 NIV). Instead, he "resolved to know nothing while [he] was with [them] except Jesus Christ and him crucified" (2:2 NIV). Moreover, though he did not communicate the gospel with eloquence and wisdom, his preaching was accompanied by "a demonstration of the Spirit's power" (2:4 NIV; the gospel itself *is* the power of God [1:18]). Paul's ultimate reason for this evangelistic approach is "that [the Corinthians'] faith might not rest on human wisdom but on God's power" (2:5 NIV). The reason human wisdom is an inadequate ground for Christian faith is not merely that the central truths of the gospel cannot be demonstrated philosophically. It is also because human rhetorical and philosophical skills can be employed effectively to *dissuade* people from accepting Christ. Those who believe a message only because of the skill of the messenger may well reject this message upon hearing a more skilled rebuttal. Hence a purely human approach is unreliable as an evangelistic strategy. The fourth and final reason Paul gives for preferring the wisdom of God to human wisdom is that the latter tends to breed arrogance on the part of its possessor, and the gospel must be received with humility (1:26–31). Pride in the attainment of wisdom and knowledge was a problem in the Corinthian church (8:1–3). It was a source of disunity among them.

These are the reasons with which Paul argues against the use of refined rhetorical and logical skills in preaching the gospel. Should we then conclude that Paul would advise Christians not to pursue a general education? This seems unlikely.

In the first place, Paul rejects human wisdom and eloquence as *evangelistic* tools (at least in some circumstances). However, evangelism is not the primary purpose of a Christian general education. Instead, Christian general learning presupposes an acceptance of the gospel and a commitment to Christ. Though Christian students' faith may not be *based* on human wisdom, they may still find human wisdom to be valuable in providing a deeper understanding of their faith and of life and the world from the standpoint of Christian faith. Second, when Paul talks about human wisdom as a point of view rather than as a set of skills, he shuns only human perspectives that are opposed to the gospel. These are the viewpoints from which "the message of the cross is foolishness" (1:18 NIV). But again, a Christian general education by its very nature is based on the gospel of Christ itself, so it does not promote a viewpoint at odds with Christian teaching. Third, Paul makes extensive use of rhetoric and logic himself throughout his epistles. This practice is no doubt a result of his personal educational history. Moreover, his use of these tools for nonevangelistic purposes indicates that his deliberate avoidance of them is restricted to his preaching of the gospel (again, at least in some circumstances). Fourth, in his address to the Epicurean and Stoic philosophers in Athens (Acts 17:15–34), Paul employed not only good reasoning and speaking skills; he also exhibited knowledge of Greek literature. Thus he seems to approve of the use of human wisdom for both the style and the substance of some of his speeches. Finally, it is important to keep in mind the rhetorical context of 1 Corinthians. Apparently, the members of the church at Corinth were excessively confident in human wisdom. What Paul says about it must be understood in the light of his desire to correct this inappropriate evaluation. Hence it would be unwarranted to take his remarks about human wisdom in 1 Corinthians to comprise his complete and unqualified assessment of it. We can conclude that Paul's discussion of human wisdom in the first four chapters of this epistle do not provide a good basis for objecting to the desirability of Christian general education.

When Paul has wisdom as "point of view" (theoretical wisdom) rather than wisdom as "reasoning and speaking skills" (practical wisdom) in mind, what he calls "human wisdom" is perhaps best interpreted as *Godless* wisdom. This is the plight of the wisdom of the Greeks apart from faith in God. However, when the wisdom that comes from general learning is based on the wisdom of God—based, that is, on Christ crucified—this sanctified human wisdom can contribute to growth in godliness. After all, our minds are gifts of God. They are part of what it is for us to be created in the image of God.

St. Paul on "Hollow and Deceptive" Philosophy

But then how should we understand Paul's warning to the Colossians: "See to it that no one take you captive through hollow and deceptive philosophy, which depends on human tradition and the elemental spiritual forces of this world rather than on Christ" (Col. 2:8 NIV)? Since philosophy in Paul's day was the source of human wisdom, and since Paul appears to be implying that the Colossians need to choose between philosophy and Christ, he seems to be advising them to avoid human wisdom altogether. But if he is, we are back to our original concern that if we follow what the Bible teaches, Christians will need to reject general learning, since it is an approach to education based (at least in part) on human wisdom.

One obvious alternative way of understanding Paul is that he is cautioning the Colossians to avoid only certain specific philosophies—those that have the negative characteristics he lists. This construal leaves open the possibility that there are philosophies that Paul would approve of, philosophies that are not hollow, deceptive, human, and worldly but rather consistent with and even supportive of Christian truths. One reason to favor this latter interpretation is that Paul seems to have a specific philosophy in mind—one that is threatening to derail the

Colossians from their Christian faith. Paul characterizes this philosophy of life to some extent in Colossians 2:16–23 as a legalistic teaching that encourages "the worship of angels" (v. 18 NIV) and promotes regulations that have only "an appearance of wisdom" (v. 23 NIV).

However, the Greek construction that Paul employs, which we have translated "hollow and deceptive philosophy," can also be rendered "philosophy and empty deceit" (NRSV). So it is unclear whether Paul is only concerned about a *particular type* of philosophy. Instead, he may be warning his hearers about philosophy *in general* along with empty deceit (by which he could mean any way of thinking that might seem full of truth but is actually devoid of it). Also, Paul likely considered any general approach to life that would have been labeled a "philosophy" during his lifetime to be counter to the Christian gospel in some way or other. There were four dominant philosophies during the Hellenistic period in which Paul lived: Cynicism, Stoicism, Epicureanism, and Skepticism. Though there are elements in each of these viewpoints with which Christians can agree, taken as a whole, they are each at odds with the Christian worldview. Paul would likely have considered Cynicism immoral, Stoicism pantheistic, Epicureanism materialistic, and Skepticism insufficiently supportive of the confidence with which Paul affirmed the supernatural elements of the Christian worldview. For these reasons, it seems likely that Paul is critical of philosophy in general, even if he has a particular philosophy in mind in his letter to the Colossians.

This interpretation of Paul does not entail that any type of education that employs philosophical reasoning is unbiblical. First, Paul may have meant by "philosophy" only a collection of beliefs, values, and practices. This leaves open the possibility that he would have approved of philosophy as an *activity* of careful and critical thinking and reasoning about the world and human life and existence. After all, he himself engaged in reasoning and argumentation, and perhaps some of it could be called "philosophical." Second, Paul might have approved of the philosophical theories constructed by later Christian philosophers such as Augustine and Thomas Aquinas if he had had an opportunity to consider them. Since their philosophical works included arguments for God's existence and other philosophical reasoning about God, Paul might consequently have seen the value of using philosophy to support Christian claims. This speculation presupposes that Paul's complaint about philosophy in general (if it was indeed about philosophy itself rather than a specific sort of philosophy) was based on the state of philosophy when he was alive, which, as suggested above, would probably have seemed entirely inconsistent with the Christian gospel during Paul's lifetime.

In any case, there are at least two ways of reading Paul's warning in Colossians 2:8 that don't require us to conclude that Paul would be opposed to Christian general education. On one of these interpretations, when Paul warns the Colossian Christians to resist captivity by philosophy, he has specific anti-Christian philosophies in mind rather than philosophy in general. On the other interpretation, though Paul has philosophy in general in mind, his admonition to shun it is based on his assumption that the specific philosophies of which he was aware, which were anti-Christian in certain important respects, were characteristic of philosophy in general, which in light of the subsequent development of Christians philosophies, we know is no longer the case.

But Paul's concerns and warnings about human wisdom in general and philosophy in particular can provide us with a helpful perspective as we prepare to think about learning for wisdom as Christians pursuing a general education. Recall that the three Old Testament books of wisdom we surveyed in Chapter Six contain the common theme that the fear of the Lord is the beginning of wisdom and that there is therefore no genuine wisdom apart from God. Given what Paul says about human wisdom, divine wisdom, and philosophy, it is clear that he also endorsed this Old Testament doctrine. What does this Pauline stance mean for our thinking about Christian general education, which draws on both human and divine wisdom? One important lesson we should learn is that we should never rely on human wisdom alone but only insofar as it is consistent with and subordinate to divine wisdom. This seems to be what the author of Proverbs has in mind when he speaks as a father to his son, urging him to "trust in the Lord with all [his] heart and lean not on [his] own understanding" (3:5 NIV).

Ministerial versus Magisterial Uses of Reason

One way to put this counsel is that we should follow Protestant reformer Martin Luther in treating human reason as "ministerial" rather than as "magisterial." That is, the role of human reason and human wisdom is to serve the purposes of God rather than the purposes of human beings (to the extent that the latter are incompatible with the former). St. Thomas Aquinas had this function of human reason in mind when he said that theology is the "queen of the sciences" and that philosophy is the "queen's handmaiden" (see Chapter Three). Human reason is magisterial rather than ministerial when people employ it in such a way as to treat it like a magistrate standing in judgment over the Christian gospel to determine whether or not it is true apart from dependence on the testimony of Scripture and the witness of the Holy Spirit. On the other hand, human reason is ministerial rather than magisterial when it is guided by God's wisdom (made available to us in his Word and through his Spirit).

Paul effectively affirms the subordinate and ministerial role of human reason in his second extant letter to the Corinthians: "We demolish arguments and every pretension that sets itself up against the knowledge of God, and we take captive every thought to make it obedient to Christ" (2 Cor. 10:5 NIV). This verse clearly implies the superiority of divine wisdom over human wisdom as well as the ministerial rather than magisterial role of human reason relative to the authority of God. Paul's statement of his ministerial use of human reason in support of the human knowledge of God also entails both a negative and a positive aim. The negative goal is the removal of intellectual obstacles to the knowledge of God. If these obstacles are *arguments*, then presumably Paul has in mind their removal by the use of counterarguments to show that the opposing arguments do not establish their conclusions. If these obstacles are *pretensions*, then presumably Paul is thinking of employing arguments to demonstrate that these claims are false. Either way, our following in Paul's footsteps would require our using human reason in the service of clearing the way for confident human knowledge of God. Paul's positive goal is the subordination of all human thought to the authority of Christ. This more constructive task necessitates not only an exercise of mind involving the articulation of a Christian worldview but also a work of the heart entailing a humble submission to Jesus as the way, the truth, and the life (John 14:6). After all, when humans exercise their reason *magisterially* in opposition to God, they not only err; they also *sin*.

As we have seen, the Old Testament wisdom writers and Paul agree that when people exercise human wisdom apart from divine wisdom, there is a danger not only of error but also of *arrogance* (and as has become clearer more recently, despair). Interestingly, this danger was recognized to some extent in ancient Greece and also among ancient Asian thinkers. We have already observed that Socrates was reluctant to consider himself wise. He was, however, willing to claim a kind of *human* wisdom that consisted in recognizing and acknowledging that his knowledge was limited. He thought he was wise only in the sense that he knew that he was relatively ignorant. Socrates compared this human wisdom with what he considered genuine wisdom, a wisdom possessed only by the gods, divine wisdom. Along with his fellow Athenians, Socrates believed it would be arrogant for a mere human being to claim to have divine wisdom. The word they used for this sort of arrogance was *hubris*, which was excessive pride shown by humans toward the gods. And as we saw in the previous chapter, the ancient Chinese sage Confucius had a similar distinction between human wisdom and divine wisdom in mind. His *Analects* consists in what he considered to be wisdom about practical human matters. But as we noted earlier, one of his disciples said, "We can hear and gather our Master's teachings in matters of knowledge and culture, but it is impossible to make him speak on the ultimate nature of things, or on the will of Heaven" (*Analects* 5:13). So Confucius, like Socrates, was aware of and respected human intellectual limitations apart from special divine revelation.

This sort of intellectual humility is unfortunately not always practiced today. Many people consider themselves wise about certain things when they are not. This intellectual overconfidence can be found in both Christian and non-Christian circles. Though it is reasonable, appropriate, and important for people to be confident when their convictions are based on adequate grounds, it is irrational, improper, and even sometimes dangerous for people to believe and promote their ideas and ideals vigorously when their experiences and evidences do not warrant their enthusiasm and zeal. These are cases in which the "heat" with which people insist on their claims exceeds the "light" by which it is possible to see that those claims are true.

Among Christians, this sort of excessive assuredness occurs when they make pronouncements about God and God's purposes and plans that go beyond what God enables us to know about him and his will on the basis of reasoning about creation and through faith in the Bible. A recurring example of this sort of overconfidence involves the announcement of a specific future date for the Second Coming of Christ. What makes this predictive practice clearly illegitimate is that, as Jesus informed us long ago, "about that day or hour no one knows, not even the angels in heaven, nor the Son, but only the Father" (Mark 13:32 NIV). Many Christians are also too sure about some assumptions about God's specific will that go beyond the general will of God clearly stated in the Bible, about interpretations of difficult passages of Scripture concerning which there is ongoing disagreement among Christians, and about rejections of well-grounded empirical scientific claims that seem to them to contradict what they take to be the clear teaching of Scripture (but are rather their fallible interpretations of what the Bible teaches).

Among some non-Christians, there can be a strident rejection of God's existence and a disparagement of religion and religious believers that surpasses what their evidence permits them to insist. One of the most salient examples of the latter sort of non-Christian intellectual arrogance is the collective attitude of the "New Atheists" toward God, religion, and religious belief. As we saw in Chapter Four, these critics of religion and religious belief make human empirical scientific reason the arbiter of all claims of knowledge and truth. But as we also saw in that context, this scientism, whether strong (entailing that all knowledge is empirical scientific knowledge) or weak (entailing that the *best* knowledge is empirical scientific knowledge) is either self-defeating (because scientism is a philosophical rather than empirical scientific claim) or unjustified (because there are clear cases of nonempirical knowledge that are superior to all empirical knowledge).

A Christian general education can help Christian students see both the extent and the limits of human knowledge. On the basis of the doctrine of creation, which includes an affirmation of our having been created in God's image, we can be confident that God has provided us with the means to know whatever God wants us to know and has revealed to us through creation, our rational insights and personal experiences, Christian tradition, and the Scriptures. But this same doctrine makes it clear that there is a vast difference between the perfect knowledge of God and the partial knowledge of human beings. So we should expect there to be things we both do not and cannot know—at least at the present time. And on the basis of the doctrine of sin, we have good reason to think that the limitations to our knowledge will be due, not only to our finitude, but also to our fallenness. As Paul says in Romans 1:18, humans suppress the truth about God because of their wickedness. That is, when we don't want to know about God because we prefer not to submit to his will, we have a tendency to doubt, downplay, and even deny the evidence God makes available to us of his existence and divine nature. And this disregard of evidence is not only irrational and arrogant; it also results in a tragic loss of opportunity to acquire wisdom about the things that matter most. In sum, a balanced biblical perspective on human knowledge that acknowledges our finitude and sinfulness will affirm both our capacity for grasping some truths and our inability to discern other truths. As Paul told the Corinthians, "Now we see only a reflection as in a mirror; then we shall see face to face" (1 Cor. 13:12a NIV). So we do see—but we don't yet see everything. And we need to exercise the humility to recognize that to be the case about ourselves.

Though our knowledge and wisdom are limited, we do know many things, and we can continue to learn many more. And if we are Christian general learners, we have a wealth of opportunities to engage in learning for wisdom of all kinds: theoretical, practical, and productive.

A Note on Sources

Two books that also discuss Paul's communication with the church at Corinth about wisdom are Richard A. Horsley's *Wisdom and Spiritual Transcendence at Corinth: Studies in First Corinthians* (Eugene: Wipf and Stock, 2008) and Timothy A. Brookins's *Corinthian Wisdom, Stoic Philosophy, and the Ancient Economy* (Cambridge: Cambridge University Press, 2014). For an introduction to the main Hellenistic philosophies, see A. A. Long's *Hellenistic Philosophy: Stoics, Epicureans, Sceptics*, 2nd ed. (Oakland: University of California Press, 1986). For an explanation and recommended contemporary application of Paul's approach with the philosophers at Athens on Mars Hill (as recorded in Acts 17), see *The Gospel in the Marketplace of Ideas: Paul's Mars Hill Experience for Our Pluralistic World* by Paul Copan and Kenneth D. Litwak (Downers Grove: InterVarsity Press Academic, 2014). In *By Philosophy and Empty Deceit* (Sheffield: Sheffield Academic Press, 1996), Troy W. Martin argues that Paul has Cynic philosophers and philosophy in mind in his letter to the Colossians. Augustine formulates an argument for God's existence in *De Libero Arbitrio* (*On the Free Choice of the Will*), book 2, and Thomas Aquinas's classic "Five Ways" to prove God's existence are contained in his *Summa Theologica*, part 1, question 2, article 3. In his *Reasonable Faith: Christian Truth and Apologetics*, 3rd ed. (Wheaton: Crossway Books, 2008), William Lane Craig discusses Martin Luther's distinction between the magisterial and ministerial uses of reason. St. Thomas Aquinas's characterization of theology as the noblest science (the "queen"), with the other sciences (including philosophy) serving as its handmaidens, can be found in his *Summa Theologica*, part 1, question 1, article 5. Socrates expresses his reluctance to consider himself wise in Plato's *Apology*, and Confucius's refusal to talk about the ultimate nature of things or on the will of Heaven was noted by his disciples—see Simon Leys, trans., *The Analects of Confucius* (New York: Norton, 1997), xxx–xxxi.

Questions for Reflection and Discussion

1. Do you agree that Paul's reported repudiation of human wisdom and eloquence when he shared the gospel with the church at Corinth does not provide Christians with a reason to avoid logic and rhetoric in general? Why or why not?

2. Do you agree that Paul's warning to the Colossians about philosophy doesn't entail that Christians should avoid philosophizing altogether? What do you think a Christian's attitude toward philosophy should be?

3. Do you agree with Luther that the role of human reason should be ministerial rather than magisterial? Why or why not? And what are some specific examples, in addition to those mentioned in the text, of both Christian overconfidence in reason and non-Christian excessive trust in reason?

SECTION THREE

LEARNING FOR WISDOM

CHAPTER NINE

LEARNING FOR THEORETICAL WISDOM

THE MAIN GOAL OF CHRISTIAN GENERAL LEARNING IS WISDOM. Wisdom is knowledge about important things—knowledge well worth having. We have seen that wisdom is multifaceted, like a diamond. There are at least three kinds of wisdom: theoretical wisdom, practical wisdom, and productive wisdom. The objects of these kinds of wisdom are truth, goodness, and beauty, respectively. Our goal in this section is to discover how learning can lead to wisdom. That is, how can our pursuit of knowledge lead to the riches of diverse kinds of wisdom? Let us begin our search with theoretical wisdom.

Theoretical Wisdom and Worldviews

Theoretical wisdom is knowledge of important truths about the nature of reality and human existence (such as the truth that there is a God who created humans in God's image). We have seen the search for this kind of knowledge among classical Greek philosophers, the writers of the Hebrew and Christian scriptures, and two ancient Asian sages.

How can a Christian general education facilitate our participation in this intellectual quest? In Chapter Five, we said that theoretical knowledge becomes theoretical *wisdom* when the knower attains a mastery of the most important truths about speculative matters. We also said that such an understanding of reality as a whole and in its various particular dimensions would constitute a worldview. Though a *complete* mastery of the truth about things is beyond our ability in this life, we can still hope to acquire as much of it as is humanly possible. We shouldn't set limits on this project prematurely, but we should acknowledge them as we find them in our journey. How can a Christian general education propel us on our way toward the goal of constructing a complete and correct worldview?

Let's first think a bit more carefully about what a worldview is. We can get a clue from the word "worldview" itself. It is a view of the world. But what is the world? The word "world" is used to mean a lot of different things. We use it to talk about both the planet Earth and the whole universe, among other things. Here we'll use it to refer to *everything that exists*, including God. So a worldview is a way of thinking about what there is. The branch of philosophy called "metaphysics" is devoted to thinking about the most general features of what there is. So philosophy will be an important aspect of learning for theoretical wisdom. As we saw in Chapter Five, Aristotle called metaphysics "first philosophy." By this he meant that it is that part of philosophy that concerns the first (most basic, fundamental, or foundational) principles or truths about what there is. Philosophers seek to discover these truths by answering the following three questions:

1. What is the world like?
2. Why does a world exist (i.e., what is the *cause* of the world—if anything)?
3. What is the place of human beings in the world?

So a worldview is at least an answer to these three metaphysical questions.

Each of these three questions can be answered fully only by means of answering other, more specific questions. As we'll see, Christians will answer at least some of these more specific questions (and thus also at least some of the more general ones) in ways different from the way non-Christians will answer them. For instance, in order to answer question 1 ("What is the world like?"), one must decide whether or not God exists. *Atheists* believe that there is no God and that only the physical universe and its contents exist (atheists are also called "naturalists," because they believe that only nature and not also anything *super*natural exists). *Theists* believe that God exists. If one concludes that there is a God, one must also seek to answer questions about God's nature ("What is God like?") and God's relation to the rest of the world ("Is God the only thing that exists—as the *pan*theists believe? If not, how is God related to everything else?").

How one answers question 2 ("Why does a world exist?") will depend on one's verdict about God. If there is a God, and if God doesn't just happen to exist but *has* to exist (because it is God's nature to exist necessarily), then one has a basis on which to figure out how to explain the existence of everything that exists. If God must exist and nothing other than God exists (i.e., if pantheism is true), then we can conclude that what there is exists because it has to. If this necessary God isn't the only reality, then it might be the case that God created everything other than God (though on one ancient view, God and the universe are distinct, eternally coexisting things, in which case God would not be the *creator* of the universe but perhaps instead only the *sustainer* of the universe). If there is no God (if atheism or naturalism is true), then there may not be an explanation of the existence of the world (though physical cosmologists may be able to explain how it is that what exists—the physical universe—reached its present configuration).

A person's response to question 3 also will rest on her reply to question 1. If God exists, then there may be an explanation of how humans fit into the big picture in terms of God. The Christian explanation of the existence of humans is that God freely created us in God's image. If

God does not exist, then there will be a very different kind of account of the relation between human beings and everything else that exists. The atheist or naturalist typically thinks of human beings as a merely accidental and purely physical by-product of the process of evolution by natural selection.

How one answers the three major metaphysical questions by answering all the subquestions that compose them will determine the general contour of one's worldview. We can divide worldviews into two main categories: naturalistic and supernaturalistic. Naturalistic worldviews deny the existence of anything beyond nature (that part of the world that is at least partially accessible to us on the basis of sensory observation). Supernaturalistic worldviews affirm the existence of something beyond nature, such as God. Worldviews that identify God with nature ("pantheistic" worldviews) are essentially naturalistic, since on that view, nothing exists outside of nature (even God, who is identical with nature on that kind of view). There are different varieties of both kinds of worldview.

What is the role of theology in the construction of a worldview? Theology is the study of God. As we saw in Chapter Three, there are two types of theology: *natural* theology and *revealed* (sacred or dogmatic) theology. Natural theology is the branch of metaphysics that raises questions about the existence and nature of God and the relation of God to everything else that exists (if anything). So natural theology is a part of philosophy. Revealed theology is a study of God that is based on God's special revelation to us in a sacred text (e.g., for Jews, the Hebrew scriptures—i.e., the Christian Old Testament; for Christians, the Bible; for Muslims, the Qur'an). Since these scriptures presuppose the existence of God, revealed theology does as well. Revealed theology can tell us things about God and God's relation to the world that we couldn't find out on the basis of unaided human reason and philosophizing. For instance, there's no way Christians could know just by philosophizing that God is a Trinity of persons and that God the Son, the Second Person of the Holy Trinity, became incarnate as Jesus of Nazareth. So what Christians find out from the Bible about God enhances their Christian worldview in important ways.

First philosophy (including natural theology) should be distinguished from what early philosophers called "natural philosophy." This is a search for wisdom about nature. Today we would call this "science" (in the sense of *empirical* science). Eventually, a distinction was made between the natural sciences and the social sciences. As we saw in Chapter Two, the former category includes at least physics, chemistry, biology, parts of psychology, and combinations of these. What ties these together is the study of things that occur naturally (without human intervention) and that are subject to observation and experiment on the basis of the senses. Physicists study the ultimate constituents of the physical or material world. Chemists investigate physical objects at the atomic and molecular levels. Biologists focus on living systems. Psychologists explore mental and behavioral phenomena. And as we also saw in Chapter Two, the social sciences consist of sociology, anthropology, economics, political science, parts of history, and combinations of these. Sociologists study the behavior of human groups, anthropologists research the aspects of human cultures, economists theorize about the exchange of goods and services among humans, political scientists describe the properties of government, and social historians investigate human history using the tools of all these social sciences. These disciplines are loosely tied together by their study of the products of human mind and will.

So a worldview is a theory about the existence and nature of things. That part of philosophy called metaphysics, including natural theology, contributes the most general truths about things. Our conclusions about these things are based on reason and observation. Revealed theology adds other things about God and God's relation to everything else. Christians accept these latter sorts of claims on the basis of faith or trust in God's testimony to us in the Bible. The sciences, both natural and social, give us a more specific picture of nature and society. Sensory experience is the source of our knowledge in this area. Are these all the academic disciplines on the basis of which we can construct a worldview? One discipline we haven't mentioned yet is mathematics. This is the science that studies numbers and magnitudes. To the extent that the truths of mathematics describe reality, we will need to include the results of mathematics in our worldview. To some extent, mathematics has already been included in virtue of the inclusion of physics, which to a large extent provides a mathematical account of the physical world.

Arthur Holmes attributes four general features to worldviews. He describes them as (1) holistic or integrational, (2) exploratory, (3) pluralistic, and (4) confessional or perspectival. To say that they are *holistic or integrational* is to say that they provide a general unifying or systematic picture of the way things are. We have already touched on their *exploratory* nature; the quest for theoretical wisdom in the form of a correct and complete worldview is a lifelong process that is never complete but always takes the form of ongoing investigation. The *pluralism* of worldviews is a function of the fact that rational, intelligent, fair-minded, and informed people will inevitably disagree with each other about some things, even if they agree about the most general things. So people can hold the same worldview at a general level and yet differ with each other on more specific ways of filling it out. A worldview is *confessional or perspectival* in that it is always based on the beliefs, values, and attitudes that constitute one's fundamental faith confession or perspective on things.

Worldviews and Unconscious Learning

So far we have been talking about worldviews as if they are always *consciously constructed*. But it is important to remember the role of unconscious learning in our acquisition of knowledge. In Chapter One, we considered some types of procedural knowledge that can be acquired on the basis of unconscious learning. Examples include a baby learning how to crawl, walk, and talk or an adult unconsciously learning how to get around her neighborhood, how to enjoy being with a particular person, or how to hum a particular tune. Much of the procedural learning we experience throughout our lives is neither deliberate nor conscious but instead just happens to and in us as we live our lives and interact with our natural and social environments. But the same thing is true of much of our recognitional learning—at least at the purely sensory level. For instance, we often learn to recognize a sound we have heard before or a smell we have smelled before merely by repeated exposure to those sensations. Of course, we don't recognize the sound as the sound *of a car horn* or the smell as the smell *of a rose* unless and until we have learned the concepts of a car horn and a rose. But conceptual learning (learning to associate a particular concept with a particular experience) need not be *fully* conscious, and even when it is, we typically subsequently employ the concepts we have learned in our acquisition of recognitional knowledge without much conscious and deliberate effort. Once people know what a car horn is, they automatically recognize the sound of one whenever they hear it—not merely as a sound but as the sound of a car horn.

What do these observations about unconscious learning have to do with worldviews? All adult human beings—even those who aren't particularly reflective or deliberate in their choices—have at least a rudimentary conception of the way the world is, of what kind of life is actually worth living, and of what kinds of things are really worth making. That is, everyone (or at least every normal and sufficiently mature human being) has something like a worldview. But if not everyone has consciously constructed a worldview, how is it that everyone has one? Since learning is a natural process made possible by our natural capacities for perception, rational intuition, and memory, we learn a lot about the world unconsciously and automatically simply by absorbing and retaining what we observe in the natural and social contexts in which we live. Our social contexts in particular (our families, neighborhoods, peer groups, schools, churches, etc.) provide us with the ways we tend to interpret and evaluate what we experience. From a sociological and anthropological standpoint, we can say that our worldviews are originally products of how our observations of the natural and social worlds are filtered through the societal and cultural lenses through which we experience these worlds. These social and cultural interpretive and evaluative frameworks influence our minds and hearts in such a way as to tend to shape and form our ideas and ideals, our perspectives and preferences, our outlooks and loves, our visions and values.

But if our worldviews are initially relatively unconscious, how can we come to know what they are so as to evaluate and revise them (if necessary)? In order to discover what we truly believe and value, we need to start by watching how we behave. Our behavior is the best clue to our values. For instance, though Jim may think and say that he loves God more than he loves anything else, if attending to his nonwork ("free time") habits reveals that he spends more time at the mall, the movies, or the sports bar than he does engaging in worship, prayer, devotional reading, Bible study, fellowship, and service, then his actions may speak louder than his words, and he may have to admit that he loves the activity that takes up the bulk of his time more than he loves God and God's Kingdom. And though Jim may think and profess that the time he spends at work is meant to bring glory to God and to contribute to the well-being of others, if a close inspection of his workday shows that he regularly behaves in self-glorying and self-serving ways, then his true motivation differs from the one he believes and says he has. Moreover, knowing what we usually do and what we really love puts us in a good position to discern what we actually believe. Jim may say he believes in a God who loves him and that he trusts God to take care of him, but if his behavior reveals that he prefers to seek solace and security in someone or something other than God, then he has reason to suspect that he doesn't really believe and trust in God after all—regardless of what he had been thinking and saying up to that point.

The more we learn about our unconscious (or subconscious) and implicit worldview, the more we are in a position to improve it in various ways. Potential improvements include replacing falsehoods with truths, articulating the implications of the truths more thoroughly, connecting those truths in systematic ways, and thinking through the extent to which the resulting system can be shown to explain life and the world more adequately than alternative systems are capable of doing. These are relatively conscious and deliberate means of striving to make our worldviews more adequate to reality as well as more coherent, systematic, unified, justified, and explanatorily powerful.

But Christians can and should also take steps to make sure that they regularly put themselves in contexts that are conducive to the support and maintenance of the Christian worldview and to avoid spending too much time in contexts that tend subconsciously and automatically to undermine their convictions, alter their values, and/or change their behaviors (or at least to be alert and guarded if they have a good reason to spend time in such contexts). Our worldviews can be transformed both consciously and deliberately through how we inform our minds and yet also unconsciously and automatically through how we allow our hearts to be formed. Consequently, we need to be vigilant to make sure that what we think and say is not at odds with what we want and do. Such a conflict between mind and heart is more prevalent than might at first seem to be the case; some students at Christian colleges and universities may sometimes love God with their minds in the classroom and during chapel but engage in practices in the residence hall and off campus (and even sometimes in the classroom and chapel!) that turn their hearts in other directions and so threaten the integrity and even the sustainability of their Christian worldview over time.

Consciously Constructing a Worldview

But let's turn back to the question about how to engage in a conscious construction of a Christian worldview (we'll return to a consideration of the importance of contexts and practices in Chapter Twelve). In the first section of this chapter, we discussed the ingredients that go into a worldview and some of the features of a worldview. How does one toss these ingredients together to get a particular picture of reality that has these features? It isn't just a matter of taking the right college courses, though this is certainly necessary and important. One also needs to make a special, ongoing effort to apply what one learns in these courses in the continual rethinking of one's worldview. If one is building a Christian worldview, this process will always be carried on from a Christian perspective, as discussed in Chapter Three ("Christian General Learning"). Since a worldview is holistic, integrational, unified, and systematic, one must always be thinking about how what one is presently learning in one area fits in with or relates to one's overall theory of the way things are. The goal is always to achieve a consistent and coherent explanation of everything. So if what you hear or read in a course conflicts with what you already think about something, you'll have to do some rethinking. Should you keep believing or valuing as you did before or should you adjust your attitude in light of your current thinking? One alters and expands a worldview bit by bit, always tinkering and making adjustments as one continues to learn and experience new things. And one will ideally continue this process for the rest of one's life.

These continual modifications of one's worldview will not only be *multi*disciplinary (involving many academic disciplines), but they will also be *inter*disciplinary (drawing on more than one discipline for a single purpose). For instance, one important question every worldview should address is what it is to be a human person. From a Christian standpoint, we can start with the (revealed, sacred, or dogmatic) theological affirmation that human beings are creatures made by God to bear his image. We can add to this consequence of the doctrine of creation another from the doctrine of sin and the Fall: humans are fallen sinners in need of salvation. Finally, we can add the doctrine of redemption: Jesus Christ died to redeem fallen humanity and to reconcile them with God for eternity. From there we can ask a philosophical question: What *kind* of thing is a human person? *Dualists* say that human persons are immaterial or nonphysical spirits or souls who have bodies. *Materialists* hold that human persons are material things (i.e., living human biological organisms). Does consistency with Christian theology require one to be a dualist? This is a question on which Christian philosophers currently disagree. Whatever the outcome of this debate, however, it is clear that Christians will need to think it through in an interdisciplinary fashion; they will need to draw on both theology and philosophy to arrive at a satisfactory view.

Moreover, it is likely that they will need to bring other disciplines to bear on this question as well. What do our best current psychological theories tell us about human nature? Do they suggest the possibility (even the necessity) of explaining human thought and behavior solely in terms of things happening in the human brain and central nervous system? If so, then there is some reason to favor the philosophical view that human persons are nothing other than biological organisms. If that is the case, then clearly the science of biology is also quite relevant to this question. Can human consciousness be explained in purely biological terms? Posing this question suggests the relevance of the social sciences (which study the products of human consciousness) to this issue. Can these sciences explain social phenomena, human cultures, political government, and economic behavior on the basis of the assumption that human persons are merely physical or material things? In order to determine whether or not they can, one must learn what sociologists, anthropologists, political scientists, and economists are saying. In the end, one must try to find an overall view of human nature that does justice both to Christian convictions and to what all the different disciplines say about human existence.

In this search, precedence must be given to one's best understanding of the doctrines of creation, sin, and redemption. The constructor of a Christian worldview cannot consistently adopt any philosophical or scientific theory that implies that humans are not created in the image of God to be free and morally responsible and capable of eternal life with God. Moreover, no Christian can rationally accept a philosophical or scientific theory that is incompatible with the possibility of God the Son becoming incarnate as a human being. However, that being said, it must be emphasized that there are a variety of competing philosophical and scientific views that are not *obviously* at odds with the

Christian faith. For instance, Christian philosophers are still debating whether the view that humans are purely material is consistent with human consciousness, freedom, and personal immortality. So the community of Christian scholars continues to converse about the contours of a Christian picture of the way things are.

As one engages in this process, it will be important to keep in mind that the people contributing to the conversation from different specific disciplines will also be approaching the issues from their own confessional stance or personal perspective. Whether such a bias is relatively conscious and well-articulated or not, everyone's thinking is substantially affected in this way. How one thinks about things will be affected, to a greater or lesser extent, by one's fundamental beliefs, values, and attitudes. Consequently, one must be aware both of how one's own conclusions are influenced by one's own basic perspective and also of how others' claims are affected by their basic perspective. With this in mind, you should try to avoid two mistakes that can easily be made. First, you must try not to reject another person's position on a particular issue simply because he or she holds a more fundamental perspective you reject. It could be that the person's more specific position is nonetheless consistent with your basic perspective. Second, you must try not to accept a claim simply because it is held by most people who have given the matter some thought. The claim could be inconsistent with your basic perspective. The rule of thumb to follow in order to avoid both of these pitfalls is that (1) you should be open to the possibility that people with basic perspectives different from yours have got the truth on some particular matter, but (2) you should also be careful to test these claims in light of your own confessional stance.

So learning for theoretical wisdom involves constructing a worldview—building a picture of the way things are. The Christian general education curriculum provides ample resources for this exercise in the form of the disciplines of philosophy (including natural theology), theology (i.e., revealed theology), the natural and social sciences, and mathematics. Ideally, the journey toward theoretical wisdom will provide you with a progressively deeper grasp of the nature of ultimate reality (including the reality of God), the universe, the earth and its inhabitants, society, and human existence. But this big picture doesn't emerge without deliberate, critical, and interdisciplinary thinking about what you're learning. A worldview doesn't just suddenly come together after one has completed a college-level course of study. Moreover, it isn't necessarily something that each and every one of your professors has in mind as an outcome of the course he or she is teaching. It is something that you have to do to some extent—even to a great extent—on your own. As a result, it will require that you find some way to be motivated to do it even though you may not be held accountable for it, and you won't be getting a grade for how well you are doing. It's an exercise for which you will need to find intrinsic rewards—you will need to discover that the search for theoretical wisdom by means of building your own worldview is an activity that you can enjoy for its own sake. This is where the heart must join with the mind in the pursuit of wisdom. You cannot become genuinely wise unless you *love* wisdom. And you can't learn to love wisdom unless you work hard at learning and at constructing a worldview as you learn. Only as your picture of reality takes shape and you begin to make sense of the world and your life will you begin to experience the satisfaction of learning various truths about the way things are.

A growing sense of the truths about these things is a necessary backdrop for the acquisition of the other two kinds of wisdom: practical and productive. Before we can be wise about how to live and what to make, we need to be wise about the world that provides us with the arena for our actions and the materials for our creations. Let us turn now to a discussion of how Christian general learning can contribute to the cultivation of practical wisdom: wisdom about how best to live our lives.

A Note on Sources

Aristotle discusses metaphysics (what he calls "first philosophy") in his *Metaphysics*. Peter van Inwagen organizes the contents of his book

Metaphysics, 4th ed. (Boulder: Westview Press, 2014) according to the three metaphysical questions discussed in this chapter. In his *Summa Theologica*, part 1, question 1, article 1, Aquinas distinguishes between philosophical science (of which natural theology is a part) and sacred doctrine (or "revealed theology," which he also labels a science). Arthur Holmes discusses the four general features of worldviews in his *The Idea of a Christian College*, revised ed. (Grand Rapids: Eerdmans, 1987), 58–59. See also his *Contours of a Christian World View* (Grand Rapids: Eerdmans, 1983). James K. A. Smith discusses the unconscious role of our cultural and social contexts in forming and shaping our worldviews in *Desiring the Kingdom* (Grand Rapids: Baker Academic, 2009).

Questions for Reflection and Discussion

1. How would you summarize what you learned in this chapter about worldviews? Given this summary, what would you say is the content of your worldview at the present time?

2. What does your behavior reveal about aspects of your worldview—what you believe and value—that are unconscious? Is what your behavior reveals about your unconscious beliefs and values at odds with what you think and say you believe and value? Explain.

3. In what ways have aspects of your worldview changed as a result of your conscious and deliberate reflection and reasoning about specific questions from an interdisciplinary perspective?

CHAPTER TEN

LEARNING FOR PRACTICAL WISDOM

In Chapter Five, we observed that the practically wise person is skilled in the art of living well. We also noted that living well involves both prudence (sagacity, shrewdness) and moral discernment. Its focus is on *action* more than it is on *thought* (though good thinking is certainly involved). Practically wise people know what is best for human beings, and they know how to live the good life. And this knowledge has special value.

The Importance of Learning for Practical Wisdom

Though each kind of wisdom is valuable, there is a sense in which practical wisdom is especially important, at least from a Christian standpoint. This is because in its absence, the other two kinds of wisdom may tend to lead to bad ends. For instance, though theoretical wisdom can be valuable in itself, the possession of it by people who lack practical wisdom may make them useless at best and arrogant at worst. Without practical wisdom, people who are theoretically wise may fail to grow personally in important ways and may also be incapable of making significant contributions to their fellow human beings—even contributions of a theoretical sort. They may spend so much time in their ivory towers that they will fail to flourish and refrain from enabling others to flourish. In the worst case, they will take such pride in their intellectual accomplishments that they will become arrogant and disdainful of those who are less enlightened. As St. Paul said to the Corinthians, "Knowledge makes arrogant, but love edifies" (1 Cor. 8:1 NASB).

Those who have productive wisdom without practical wisdom may suffer from an inability to discern which objects are most worth making. Without the knowledge, provided by practical wisdom, of what is best for human beings, people will lack the perspective required to know what kinds of productions are conducive to that end. What they make may then be, at best, useless, and at worst, harmful. Moreover, without the moral focus of practical wisdom, beauty and benefit may take a back seat to whatever is novel and untried, including what is not merely ugly but also grotesque, shameful, demeaning, and dehumanizing. In sum, theoretical and productive wisdom must be accompanied by practical wisdom to avoid these potential ill effects. Moreover, practical wisdom itself must maintain its moral center, without which it may degenerate into mere cleverness, or at worst, the wiliness, slyness, or craftiness of the con man or criminal. Such people would know how to live in such a way as to accomplish their evil or wicked ends, but they would not know how to live well or how to help others to live well. It is clear that a Christian general education must include the responsible cultivation of practical wisdom.

Whereas the goal of theoretical wisdom is simply to know the truth about important things, the goal of practical wisdom is to live a good life. Wisdom, then, involves both theories and practices. Practical wisdom is knowledge of how to apply theory to practice. More specifically, it is knowledge of how to apply theories about human nature and the meaning of human life to the practice of living well. The practically wise person knows what human life is all about and also knows how to live a human life in conformity with that knowledge. So practical wisdom is a combination of declarative knowledge (knowing that) and procedural knowledge (knowing how). As such, it is a wisdom that melds the mind and the heart. It is a wisdom that entails both learning and loving, both loving to learn and learning to love. Loving to learn requires loving the truth, since knowledge of the truth is the outcome of learning. Learning to love involves knowing what is good—knowing what things are really worth loving and knowing how to love them.

Practical Wisdom and the Great Chain of Being

All good things are worth loving, but some things are better than other things, so some good things deserve to be loved more than other good things do. The practically wise person knows the truths about the degrees of goodness things have and thus also knows how much it is appropriate to love them.

So practical wisdom requires knowing how much goodness or value things possess in order to know how much these things merit being loved. We can look to the thought of St. Augustine to provide us with a basis for this kind of knowledge. Augustine followed Plato and later philosophers in the platonic tradition in believing that everything that exists or has being or reality is good just in virtue of the fact that it exists. That is, positive value is a part of the fabric of reality. Moreover, he agreed with the Platonists that things of different kinds have different degrees of reality and different degrees of positive value corresponding to those different degrees of reality. Accordingly, everything that exists can be placed in a hierarchy from those things that have the least amount of reality and goodness all the way up to that which has the most reality and goodness. Since God is a perfect and infinite or unlimited being, God has the highest degree of reality and goodness. Moreover, God created the rest of the world to have varying degrees of reality and goodness. Nonliving, inorganic things are in the category of things having the lowest degree of reality and goodness. Plants are a step up in the hierarchy or chain. That's because they not only *exist*, like rocks, but they are also *alive*. Living things are more real and thus more valuable than nonliving things. Perhaps you can see how this goes now. Animals are better than plants and rocks, since animals not only exist and live but have other valuable properties as well. Unlike plants, animals can gather information about their environments by means of sense organs, and they can move around these environments on the basis of this sensory information so as to find food for themselves and avoid being food for other animals. We human beings are at the top of the terrestrial chain, since we have all the characteristics of those things lower down (we exist, we live, we can sense and move around), and we also can think and choose rationally—that is, on the basis of reasons. Our rationality both distinguishes us from the rest of God's creation on Earth and makes us superior in value to those things. Perhaps it seems a bit odd to say that we have more *reality* than everything else does. The same point can be made by saying that we possess all the general characteristics that make the things lower than us in the hierarchy valuable and that we also have additional general characteristics that add even more value to our nature. This is what makes humans superior in worth to every other created terrestrial kind of thing.

If Augustine's "Great Chain of Being" picture of reality is correct, then it can give us theoretical wisdom about the way things are. It can also contribute to the possession of practical wisdom by providing the primary basis on which we can make wise decisions about how to live our lives. Let's follow Augustine's thought a bit more to see how this works. Augustine characterizes a sinful life as a life consisting of "disordered loves." A disordered love life is a life lived on the basis of loving things either more or less than they ought to be loved given their actual degree of reality and value—their position on the Great Chain of Being. The particular kinds of sins can be explained in terms of specific wrong ways of loving. For instance, greed involves loving something nonliving (money) more than it deserves to be loved. Gluttony is a matter of loving some living things (food) too much, and lust is the illegitimate loving of other human beings (loving their bodies more than their souls). Loving oneself too much constitutes the sin of pride. Pride can be manifested in the form of either loving oneself more than other persons who deserve to be loved *as much* (in the case of other human beings) or more than someone who deserves to be loved *more* (in the case of God). Augustine's general name for this wrong kind of love is "cupidity." The first step on the road to living a sinless life, and thus having a properly ordered love life, is to love God more than you love anything else. After all, in virtue of his place on top of the Great Chain of Being, God deserves to be the highest object of our love. The next step is to learn to love other things as they ought to be loved, given their degree of value. So for instance, one should love human souls more than money, food, or human bodies. In this way, one will avoid hurting people out of greed, gluttony, lust, and so on. Moreover, we should, as Jesus instructs us, love our neighbors as we love ourselves. After all, our neighbors are fellow human beings, and we therefore occupy the same level of the Great Chain of Being. Augustine's word for this proper kind of loving is "charity." Since the practically wise person not only knows what the true value of things is but also makes decisions about how to relate to things based on their true value, the ideally practically wise person will be a person who exhibits charity rather than cupidity.

In Chapter Four ("Wisdom in the Ancient Greek Tradition"), we said that the philosopher Aristotle held that practical wisdom and moral virtue go hand in hand: he thought it isn't possible for a person to have one without the other. We can now see why this is the case. First, let's see why practical wisdom always involves moral virtue. Practical wisdom involves knowing how to live well. Living well requires personal fulfillment. One can be fulfilled only if one learns to live a life characterized by right loving (charity) instead of a life marked by sinful, wrong loving (cupidity). This is because a sinful life is a miserable life. Only a godly, holy, righteous life involving loving God above all else and loving everything else as it should be loved can make a person happy, fulfilled, and (eventually) blissful. So practical wisdom involves knowing how to have a charitable heart. A person with a charitable heart is a morally virtuous person. So a practically wise person is a morally virtuous person. We can also see how moral virtue always goes along with practical wisdom. A morally virtuous person is a person who has a virtuous character. A person with a virtuous character is a person who knows how to live virtuously. A person who knows how to live virtuously is a person who knows how to be fulfilled and happy—how to live well. But that kind of person is a person with practical wisdom. So you can't be morally virtuous without being practically wise (and vice versa).

Proper loving is a matter of the mind and the will. As a matter of the mind, it involves knowing how to make decisions on the basis of wisdom about the true values of things, as discussed above. As a matter of the will, it involves being able to choose rightly on the basis of this wisdom. Given how Augustine characterizes right loving or choosing, this means having the ability not to sin. But according to Christian doctrine, only God can enable us not to sin. Only God can effect a conversion of our will so as to enable us to live a life of charity as opposed to a life of cupidity. In order to accomplish this, God has to transform our hearts completely. He has to change our characters from being habitually sinful to being disciplined in godly loving. The process in which God changes our hearts, wills, and characters in this way is the lifelong process of "sanctification." It is the process by means of which God sanctifies us or makes us holy. This process is entirely a work of God's Holy Spirit, though it requires our submission and cooperation. Consequently, since practical wisdom requires moral virtue, and complete moral virtue isn't possible without God's supernatural work in our lives, it follows that one cannot be completely practically wise without God's intervention in his or her life. If this is the case, then what could possibly be the role of a Christian general education in the acquisition of practical wisdom? How can Christian general learning contribute to the cultivation of wisdom about how to live well?

Practical Wisdom and the Academic Disciplines

Though only God's supernatural intervention can change a sinful will into a righteous one, it is possible for us to use our natural God-given minds to learn more and more about how to exercise our transformed wills in wise ways. Here's where a Christian general education can be a valuable asset. Practical wisdom provides an intellectual basis for the deliberation and decision that leads to good individual and corporate policy making, action, and evaluation. General learning can enrich this foundational wisdom by drawing on those disciplines or parts of disciplines that have most to do with turning theory into practice. What are these disciplines? Both philosophy and theology contain components dedicated to the study of moral or ethical values, character, and behavior. The difference between the two is simply that moral philosophy draws on human reason for wisdom about right and wrong, good and bad, whereas Christian moral theology is an attempt to discern what the Bible teaches about these things. In addition to philosophy and theology, other disciplines that can help one be more practically wise include the natural and social sciences and the humanities—especially literature. In the rest of this section, we will discuss more specifically the ways in which each of these disciplines can play a role in helping a heart transformed by God be wiser.

One difference between philosophy and theology on the one hand and the natural and social sciences on the other hand is that the former disciplines yield *normative* theories, whereas the latter disciplines provide *descriptive* theories. That is, philosophers and theologians discuss the ways in which human beings *ideally ought* to live their lives, whereas natural scientists describe the *actual* features of the natural world, and social scientists discuss the ways in which people *actually do* live their lives. Practical wisdom requires knowledge of both kinds (normative and descriptive). For instance, a practically wise person needs to know not only what constitutes a properly ordered love life but also what the world is like, how it needs to be and can be changed, and what the most efficient and effective ways of bringing about those changes are. Where philosophy and theology can help one be wise about the *norms* on the basis of which we ought to behave and evaluate behavior, only the descriptive sciences can help us determine the *facts* about how far the world falls short of these norms and how we might work to bring it into line with them.

Practical wisdom includes not only wisdom about how to be morally good but also wisdom about how to live in such a way as to maximize other important values. Here we are using the word "value" in the sense of something sought after as an ideal end or goal. A genuinely good value is one that *ought* to be the object of our efforts, whether it actually is or not. Among these values, in addition to moral ones, are social and political goods like mutual understanding and appreciation, cooperation, social harmony, friendship, distributive justice (making sure everyone gets the good things they deserve to get), liberty (freedom from undue governmental constraints), and equality. There are also general practical values that aren't necessarily moral values but that can contribute to the fostering of moral, social, and political values. These include efficiency (using resources wisely) and effectiveness (reliably bringing about the goals that our actions are intended to produce).

All these values—and their opposites, such as injustice, disharmony, inefficiency, and so on—are products of individual and corporate action. They all arise out of what people do, whether alone or together. Moreover, intentional actions are the result of choice or decision. Choices come about by means of an exercise of will. Except in the case of habitual or automatic behavior, this exercise of will comes about after a period of deliberation in which the individual or group considers alternative courses of action and the reasons for and against them. It is during this process of deliberation that practical wisdom is needed. It is only during this stage in the history of an action that people are sufficiently engaged in rational reflection to make good use of knowledge about what ends are most worth striving to realize and what means are most likely to bring them about in the desired way.

Let's turn now to a consideration of how the different academic disciplines can be brought to bear on the cultivation of the practical wisdom needed for fruitful individual and corporate deliberation and decision. As we think about this, it is important to remember that practical wisdom and moral virtue go hand in hand. The goal of Christian general learning here is to produce people who are both wise and good—people whose heads and hearts are attuned to work together to enable them to love and serve God and all of God's creation as they should. Arthur Holmes provides a helpful discussion of ways in which the disciplines comprising a Christian general education can each contribute to the teaching of moral decision-making. We will summarize his suggestions and then give examples to illustrate his recommendations. Holmes focuses on four areas of the curriculum: (1) the natural and social sciences, (2) biblical studies and Christian theology, (3) philosophy, and (4) the remaining humanities (history, literature, and the arts).

Holmes assigns the natural and social sciences the role of providing many of the cases that call for moral decision. Examples of such cases would include cases involving nuclear weaponry, global warming, genetic engineering, addictive behavior, juvenile delinquency, gambling, political corruption, and so on. Holmes thinks of these empirical sciences as potentially making four kinds of contributions in our thinking about these (and other) sorts of cases: (a) providing an understanding of the facts in such cases that require moral evaluation and decision, (b) articulating alternative ways to respond to these cases, (c) projecting the likely short-term and long-range consequences of these alternatives, and (d) analyzing the values and expectations of practitioners in their fields. In sum, the natural and social sciences can help us identify specific areas in which moral decisions need to be made, and they can provide us with the descriptive scientific resources we need to make these decisions wisely.

As for biblical studies and theology, Holmes sees these areas as the basis for general moral principles (e.g., "The highest human good is to love, serve, and glorify God," and "We should love our neighbors as we love ourselves"), specific moral rules (e.g., "killing is wrong," and "adultery is wrong"), "control" beliefs (e.g., beliefs about the purpose of government and beliefs about the purpose of marriage), and moral exemplars (especially Jesus). Moreover, he points out that the history of Christian ethical thinking is a rich resource for contemporary reflection.

We will divide the contributions Holmes attributes to philosophy into two categories: skill and content. As for skills, philosophy can help students clarify concepts and analyze, evaluate, and construct arguments. It can also help students organize their thinking. As for content, the history of philosophy contains an ample set of moral theories: theories about the nature of what is right and good. More recently, philosophers have also written quite a bit in the area of applied ethics, taking ethical theories and applying them to various moral problems and dilemmas. They have also taken a renewed interest in the important role of character and virtue in the moral life. As a consequence of these philosophical developments, there are many valuable philosophical resources currently available that address questions about moral duties, the morally relevant consequences of human behavior, and the virtues that contribute to a morally good character.

Finally, Holmes draws together the disciplines of history, literature, and the arts as tools to help students interpret the human condition. Thinking about the past, reading a novel, and enjoying an artwork can all be ways in which students can be provided with deeper insights into moral problems, agents, and decisions. These disciplines are also especially good at providing a realistic picture of what it is to be human in thought, feeling, and action. They present life with all its complexities, tensions, and ambiguities. These areas of study also stimulate the imagination and broaden a person's sympathies. They can open students' minds and hearts to people who are different from them in various ways, enabling them to deepen their understanding and appreciation of them.

The role of these four areas of the Christian general education curriculum in wise Christian thinking about moral issues for deliberation and decision can be illustrated by a few examples. Contributions of the empirical sciences to conversations about *some* moral issues are relatively uncontroversial. For instance, in the late 1970s, scientists began to observe a steady depletion of the ozone layer in the Earth's atmosphere that protects living things from damaging ultraviolet rays. They eventually determined this O_3 depletion was being caused by human-made halocarbon refrigerant emissions and that it was resulting in damage to biological organisms, including skin cancer in human beings. Most of the world's nations took steps, on the basis of this scientific knowledge, to prohibit the use of ozone-depleting substances. As a result, scientists have observed that the process of ozone depletion has been halted, and many expect it to be reversed.

In contrast, the contribution of the empirical sciences to discussions of global warming is controversial. Though most people agree that the average temperature of the Earth's atmosphere and oceans is on the rise, many dispute the claims of climate scientists that increasing concentrations of greenhouse gasses produced by human activities (such as deforestation and fossil fuel burning) are accelerating this global warming trend. Many also contest scientific forecasts of dire consequences for the Earth and its inhabitants if human-caused CO_2 emissions are not decreased substantially. Among the factors that complicate this debate is a conflict of values. Though the opposed parties agree to value human welfare, they disagree about the relative importance of environmental and economic factors. If a reduction of CO_2 emissions to save the environment is likely to have negative consequences for the global economy, then policy makers will need to make hard choices about the best way to promote human well-being. Clearly theoretical wisdom based on both the natural and social sciences is needed as a basis for practically and morally wise decisions about how best to respond to global warming.

Though there is much agreement among Christians about the *general* contribution of Scripture and theology to our moral deliberations and decisions, there isn't a consensus about how best to apply biblical teaching when it comes to certain specific "hot button" issues. For instance, Christians can agree with each other that the Bible teaches us that we ought to take care of the poor but disagree with each other about how best to do so (by tax-supported government welfare programs or by voluntary giving to private charitable institutions). Moreover, Christians can agree that the Bible teaches that sexual activity should take place only in the context of lifelong heterosexual marriage but disagree about whether homosexual couples should be legally allowed to marry. A Christian general education ought to equip students to interpret the Bible rightly and to apply its teachings wisely in their attempts to be faithful to God in what they think and how they live when it comes to moral and social issues such as these. However, it seems unlikely that even the best preparation of this sort will guarantee that Christians will come to a complete agreement about how we should act on the basis of biblical teaching.

The contribution of philosophy to conversations about these issues (stewardship of creation, care for the poor, the covenant of marriage) will involve clarifying key concepts (e.g., benefit and harm, liberty and welfare, justice and rights), formulating and evaluating arguments (e.g., for and against alternative public policy proposals), and facilitating thinking about relevant moral duties (e.g., to protect and promote human welfare, freedom, and rights), relevant morally significant consequences of alternative courses of action (e.g., environmental integrity or destruction, economic growth or decline, social welfare or harm), and relevant moral virtues and values (e.g., responsibility, compassion, respect).

Among the roles of history, literature, and the arts will be the provision of concrete narrative accounts and symbolic portrayals of relevant actual and possible human interactions with the natural and social worlds. Such stories and representations can provoke one's imagination and stimulate one's desires in ways that can encourage concern about environmental degradation, sympathy for and indignation over the suffering and unjust treatment of fellow human beings, and sorrow for the profane disregard of what is sacred. Many have had the experience of seeing others in a new light after hearing their personal stories and of coming to care about the plight of a disadvantaged group through getting to know them and their difficult circumstances. Clearly, both hearing about and hearing from others can increase our concern for them and for people like them. And *artful* stories and portrayals of suffering and injustice can be especially effective in helping shape a heart of practical wisdom.

This chapter began with an emphasis on the importance of learning for practical wisdom. Practically wise people know how to use their theoretical wisdom to live in ways that serve others and glorify God. They also know how to employ their productive wisdom to make things that help and enrich their fellow human beings and that bring honor to their Maker. In addition, those who are practically wise know how to love God and the things God created in ways appropriate to the relative value of these objects of their love. Thus they know how to love God with all their hearts, souls, minds, and strength; how to love their neighbors as they love themselves; and how to love everything else in God's good creation in a manner and to the extent that fits the natures of those things. Moreover, with God's ongoing assistance through the Holy Spirit, practically wise Christians can become gradually more successful in being able consistently to put this procedural knowledge into practice. As those who follow Christ continue to cooperate with the Holy Spirit in this endeavor of moral transformation, their hearts will be changed, and they will progressively want only what God wants. When this godly motivation is combined with the theoretical wisdom acquired through their Christian general education, Christian students will become better able to make wise moral, social, and political decisions. We have seen that the entire general education curriculum—the natural and social sciences, biblical studies and theology, philosophy, history, literature, and the arts—can contribute to this decision-making ability. We saw that one of the ways literature and the arts can facilitate such deliberation is by portraying destruction, harm, and wrongdoing so as to highlight the irresponsibility, injustice, and wickedness that need to be resisted. But in order for the storytellers and artists to be able to write and depict the plight of a ruined creation and of its suffering and violated creatures well, these wordsmiths and artisans must learn to be *productively* wise.

A Note on Sources

The idea of reality as a Great Chain of Being is rooted in Plato (see especially his *Republic*) and Aristotle (see his *On the Soul*) and developed by the Neoplatonist Plotinus (see his *Enneads*) and then Augustine (in works of his such as *On the Free Choice of the Will*, *Confessions*, and *Enchiridion*). Augustine's account of sin as disordered love is based on his assumption of the Great Chain of Being and is developed in his *Confessions*. See also Arthur O. Lovejoy, *The Great Chain of Being: A Study of the History of an Idea* (Cambridge: Harvard University Press, 1976). Arthur Holmes's discussion of the contribution of the Christian general education disciplines to the teaching of moral decision-making can be found in his *Shaping Character: Moral Education in the Christian College* (Grand Rapids: Eerdmans, 1990). Edward A. Parson discusses the history of international efforts to protect the ozone layer in his *Protecting the Ozone Layer: Science and Strategy* (Oxford: Oxford University Press, 2003). For more on global warming, see Mark Maslin's *Global Warming: A Very Short Introduction*, 2nd ed. (Oxford: Oxford University Press, 2009).

Questions for Reflection and Discussion

1. Do you agree that learning for practical wisdom is essential in a Christian general education? Why or why not?

2. Do you find Augustine's characterization of sin in terms of disordered loves and his account of properly ordered loves in terms of the Great Chain of Being helpful? Why or why not?

3. In addition to those given in the text, what example(s) would you add of drawing on the Christian general education disciplines to make practically wise decisions about how to solve problems that face human beings?

CHAPTER ELEVEN

LEARNING FOR PRODUCTIVE WISDOM

Colleges, Christian and otherwise, are typically devoted to the study of the *arts* and sciences. The sciences are academic disciplines devoted primarily to the purpose of acquiring propositional knowledge about the world. The arts, on the other hand, are practices that aim at the production of things of various kinds. In short, the sciences are for knowing and the arts are for making. But in spite of these different goals, these two human activities are similar in certain respects. Just as there are scientists (people) who engage in science (a set of skills) in order to produce science (theories about specific aspects of the world), so also there are artists (people) who engage in art (skills) to produce art (works).

The Nature and Variety of Artworks

In everyday speech these days, the word "art" tends to apply narrowly to the sorts of works one is likely to find in an art museum and to the skill possessed by the people who make those kinds of things. For present purposes, however, we will include in the "artwork" category *anything people deliberately make for a purpose*. Probably a better word is "artifact." We'll use these words interchangeably. We can divide up the things that exist in the world into two categories: (1) natural objects and (2) artifacts. Natural objects would exist even if people did not. For instance, there would still be rocks, trees, and animals even if there weren't any human persons. But artifacts depend for their existence not only on the existence of human persons but also on those persons intentionally producing those things. Certainly the category of artifacts includes paintings, poems, and sculptures. However, it also includes tables, chairs, and computers.

These examples illustrate how an artwork or artifact is *anything* people deliberately make for a purpose. So both the various works of the *fine arts* (artworks produced primarily to be enjoyed) and the products of the *practical arts* (artworks made mostly for the function they fulfill) are artifacts. The former category consists more specifically in at least the visual arts (e.g., painting, sculpture), the literary arts (e.g., poetry, creative writing), and the performing arts (e.g., music, theater, dance). The latter category (the practical arts) can be further divided into the *productive* practical arts (e.g., carpentry, cookery, and masonry) and the *cooperative* practical arts (e.g., farming, medicine, and teaching). The former practical arts have to do with making things that don't already exist in nature (e.g., houses, cooked meals, and fireplaces) and the latter practical arts concern cooperating in the production of the sorts of things that do occur naturally (e.g., food, health, and knowledge).

Both the fine arts and the practical arts yield products that are concrete, particular, physical things and products that are abstract, universal, nonphysical things. In the fine arts category, an example of the former sort of artwork is Michelangelo's *David* sculpture, which is situated in the Accademia Gallery in Florence, Italy. Though there are replicas of this statue elsewhere (such as in the Victoria and Albert Museum in London, England), only the statue in the Accademia is the genuine *David*. An example of the latter sort of artifact (abstract, universal, and nonphysical) that is in the fine arts classification is Handel's

Messiah oratorio. In this case, this artwork produced by Handel is *abstract* because it is not identical with any particular inscribed score and libretto (text) that represents it, it is *universal* because it is one thing that can be realized in many particular instances, and it is nonphysical because it consists essentially in a combination of musical and literary *ideas*. Of course, each individual *performance* of the *Messiah* is a concrete, particular, physical event, but the *Messiah* itself is distinct from performances of it. In the practical arts, there are also concrete, particular, physical artifacts (e.g., computers) and abstract, universal, nonphysical ones (e.g., computer programs).

In saying that artworks or artifacts are anything *people deliberately make*, you should keep in mind that the people in question work either individually (as poets often do) or collectively (as automobile manufacturers usually do). Moreover, *intentional* rather than *accidental* causation is required. Though someone can cause a wine glass to break by inadvertently dropping it on the floor, we do not think of the resulting collection of shattered glass as a work of either fine or practical art (though a person can subsequently decide to make it one). Additionally, an artwork is something people *make* or produce. Strictly speaking, no human being is capable of genuinely *creating* anything, since creation involves bringing something into existence out of nothing—that is, without using any preexisting material. Only God can do that. So what people do is make or produce things by imposing forms on other things. Finally, an artwork must be produced deliberately *for a purpose* (either simply to enjoy it or to use it for some other purpose). Therefore, though the footprint you leave in the sand while you are walking is something you make, it is not necessarily something you make *for a purpose* (though it could be).

Learning for Productive Wisdom about Artworks

Now that we have thought carefully about the nature and variety of artworks or artifacts, we are in a position to discuss learning for the kind of wisdom that applies to them. In Chapter Five, we said that productive wisdom is based on three kinds of knowledge: (1) propositional knowledge about what general characteristics make objects beautiful and/or useful, (2) recognitional knowledge of beautiful and useful things as opposed to ugly and useless things (knowing them when you see them), and (3) procedural knowledge that consists in knowing how to make worthwhile (beautiful and/or useful) artifacts. An ideally and so maximally productively wise person will have mastered all three of these kinds of knowledge—at least with respect to a specific kind of artwork or area of art. One way to think about maturing, developing, or growing as an artist, artisan, craftsperson, or engineer is in terms of increasing one's degree of productive wisdom in a specific art, craft, or type of design and/or manufacturing.

Now of course a Christian college or university is not a trade, vocational, technical, or occupational school. These latter sorts of institutions tend to be focused relatively narrowly on training apprentices in a particular skill, craft, or trade. Nor is a Christian college or university an academy, conservatory, or professional school. These places are dedicated to providing a specialized education for artists, musicians, and preprofessionals. Instead, a Christian college or university offers its students a *general* education aimed primarily at the dissemination of *universal knowledge* and *comprehensive wisdom*. That is, a Christian general education is meant, at least ideally, to enable students to acquire and cultivate the intellectual virtues (mental abilities) potentially possessed by *all* normal human beings (regardless of their occupation or profession) for the sake of gaining all kinds of knowledge (propositional, recognitional, procedural) about every academic discipline, with the goal of becoming a person characterized by every sort of wisdom (theoretical, practical, and productive). In short, a Christian general education is primarily intellectual. But the intellectual resources (intellectual virtue, knowledge, wisdom) it encourages its students to develop are ultimately intended to make possible a life characterized by broad understanding, loving service, and fruitful production—all to the glory of God.

So the contribution of a Christian general education to the cultivation of productive wisdom will involve teaching that facilitates acquiring the three types of knowledge mentioned above that serve as the ingredients of this sort of wisdom. Recall that the first type of knowledge that contributes to productive wisdom is propositional knowledge that enables its possessor to *understand* artworks. Much of this type of knowledge can be acquired by means of thinking in terms of Aristotle's "four causes." Aristotle believed that we could give a complete explanatory account of any type of thing, whether a natural object or an artifact, by answering four questions about it: What is it? What's it made of? How was it made? And what's it for? The answers to these four questions will give us explanatory propositional knowledge about an artwork that will contribute to our productive wisdom about it.

Let's see how this works in the case of Michelangelo's *David*. Clearly, the answer to Aristotle's first question is that this work of art is a sculpture or statue of the biblical personage David. This answer tells us what *kind* of thing the *David* is. Aristotle, following his teacher Plato, says that something is of a certain kind in virtue of its *form*. By "form," Aristotle does not necessarily mean "shape," although in some cases the form of something is at least to some extent a function of its physical shape (e.g., a brick). Nor does he necessarily mean *how the material that composes the thing is organized*, though this is getting closer to what he has in mind. For our purposes, we can think of the form of something, or its "formal cause," as *that into which something is made.*

But what is this "something" that Michelangelo made into a sculpted statue of David? That is, what is the material, stuff, or "matter" that composes this artwork? That's what Aristotle's second question is asking. And of course the answer in this case is "marble." So marble is the "material cause" of this statue. It is *that out of which something (the statue) is made.* And now that we know what this sculpture's formal and material "causes" are, we understand something important about it. We know about a couple of things that cause it to be what it is—a marble statue of David.

But we can learn more about it by asking Aristotle's third question: How was it made? In asking this question, we are inquiring about what Aristotle would call the sculpture's "efficient" cause. The efficient cause of something is *that by means of which it is made*. Of course, the short answer to this question is "Michelangelo." But a more complete response would specify Michelangelo's thought process (his "productive ideas"), his artistic skill as a sculptor, and the tools he uses (including his own hands) to employ this skill on the basis of this thought process to (gradually) produce the *David*.

The fourth and final question we need to address to understand this sculpture, according to Aristotle, is "What is it for?" or "*Why* is Michelangelo making it?" An answer to this query will tell us what the statue's *final* cause is. It will indicate *that for the sake of which it is made*. This question may be the most difficult of the four to answer, since Michelangelo may have had more than one purpose for making the *David*, his reasons may have been complex, and we may not be in a position to discern what his motives were in their entirety. This question may also be the one of the four that is of most interest to art historians, who seek to interpret and evaluate works of art within their historical contexts relative to the intentions of the artists who produce them. In the case of the *David*, such interpretations may seek to account for Michelangelo's choice to sculpt it in psychological, sociological, political, economic, and/or cultural terms (e.g., he wanted to create something beautiful and meaningful, please his peers, make a political statement, make money, and promote the values of Florence). These interpretations may also attempt to explain the more specific production and aesthetic choices Michelangelo made in designing the *David* and executing his design (e.g., he wanted to provide an artistic response of a certain kind to Donatello's earlier *David* statue). And explanations of both of these sorts could appeal both to Michelangelo's conscious thoughts and desires and also to external social influences of various sorts that influenced him subconsciously.

Now an account of an artifact in terms of Aristotle's four causes of the sort just sketched does not necessarily answer *all* the questions we might have about it when we are seeking to understand it as fully as possible. However, such an overall explanation certainly can contribute significantly to our propositional knowledge of at least four important aspects of the work. Moreover, theoretical knowledge of the nature, composition, production, and purpose of an artwork can also facilitate our evaluation, criticism, and appreciation of the work and others that are like it in relevant respects. Of course, such evaluation presupposes the existence of a standard or standards relative to which the evaluation is made. And it is notoriously controversial whether there are any standards of this sort that are universal (so that they apply to works in all times and places) and objective (so that they are not merely a matter of subjective personal taste or preference). Is beauty merely in the eye of the beholder? Christians, who believe that God is the source of all truth, goodness, and beauty, have a reason for thinking that the answer to this question is no. But even so, important questions remain to be answered about cultural differences that might determine different specific ways in which more abstract universal and objective aesthetic standards are realized in various human contexts.

So propositional knowledge of the sort we have been discussing about artifacts informs our evaluation and appreciation of them. It can also facilitate our *recognitional* knowledge concerning them. That is, the more we know about artworks, the more we will be able to recognize the characteristics that make them more or less aesthetically valuable and/or useful when we experience them. Propositional knowledge of the appropriate kind may not be *necessary* for recognitional knowledge of this sort; people can have the ability to recognize the relative value or disvalue of an artwork on the basis of *intuition*. However, there is good reason to think that propositional knowledge can enhance recognitional knowledge in this area. At the very least, the former sort of knowledge can enable a person to articulate, explain, and justify a particular judgment of artistic value or utility. The productively wise person will be in possession of *both* kinds of knowledge.

The fully productively wise person will also know how to *make* worthwhile things. That is, he or she will have the procedural knowledge required to produce artifacts. Now of course every actual work of art is a work of a *specific type* of art, such as filmmaking or bridge building. So the knowledge required for producing something will be a specialized form of knowledge. Such knowledge is often also relatively "tacit" or implicit in the sense that it cannot be, or cannot easily be, explicitly articulated. And because productive procedural knowledge is both relatively specialized and tacit, it is best acquired by apprenticing oneself to a "master" of a particular art, under whose direction one observes how works of a certain kind are produced and also attempts to imitate the skilled work that one witnesses. One is unlikely to be able to achieve mastery of an art simply by reading a manual that records a description of productive processes and sets of instructions for making things.

With the need for such specialized apprenticeship in mind, one may wonder what a Christian college or university could offer as a relatively general preparation for the skilled making of artworks. Is the combination of propositional and recognitional knowledge of artifacts the only contribution to productive wisdom that a Christian general education can provide? Must "how to" productive knowledge be acquired in educational settings with narrower focuses? Not necessarily. For one thing, whatever general skills all productive skills share in common could be legitimate objects of general instruction. Such "transferable" skills could include perceiving, imagining, inventing, organizing, measuring, evaluating, and designing. Moreover, even more specific productive skills, such as oratory (public speaking), painting, sculpting, acting, singing, writing (of particular types of works, such as poetry), programming, and creating a business plan can be appropriately acquired and refined in a Christian general education context at least as concrete illustrations and examples of the application of general productive principles and procedures. Finally, the contemporary common and nearly universal practice in colleges and universities of requiring students to *major* in a particular field means that a general education today is typically a combination of general and special instruction. Generally educated students have an intellectual experience that is both generally broad and specifically deep. Though this hybrid or mixed approach may not result in a "pure" general education of the traditional sort, it is nonetheless the practical reality with which most general educators and students are working today. And instruction in a specific productive skill or skill set is an appropriate component of specialized major study.

Productive Wisdom and the Christian General Education Curriculum

We'll end this chapter with some reflections about how various areas and disciplines within the Christian general education curriculum can make contributions to learning for productive wisdom. Let's return to Aristotle's four causes to aid us in our thinking about potential disciplinary resources of this sort. When we make things, we employ natural materials (or materials ultimately composed of natural materials) as ingredients. Moreover, it is obvious that each specific kind of material is suitable to be made into some types of artifacts but not others. Wood can be made into a chair but not into fountain, and vice versa for water. What makes a type of material appropriate for some productive purposes but not for others is that it has some specific properties and lacks other specific properties.

When the material is *physical* (rather than nonphysical, as in the ideas that go into a novel), the physical sciences can provide valuable knowledge about what properties of various types of materials make them suitable for some productive purposes but not for others. And the branch of the physical sciences that is especially helpful for this purpose is what has come to be known, appropriately, as "materials science." Though this is a relatively specialized area of the physical sciences, it draws heavily on more general physical scientific knowledge of the sort one can learn in a general education setting. So the natural, physical sciences can contribute to one sort of knowledge on which productive wisdom is based by providing productively wise people with information about the properties that make physical materials suitable for some forms and purposes but not for others.

But as we pointed out above, though some artifacts are physical things, others are not. And in the case of the latter, the "material" out of which they are made is, perhaps paradoxically, not *physical* but instead *non*physical material. A poem is a clear example of an artwork that consists of only nonphysical ingredients. The ingredients of a poem are the language (words, sentences, etc.) of which the poem consists and the meaning (concepts, ideas) that language expresses (and sometimes the way the poem's words look or are arranged when it is printed or how the words sound when they are spoken). Though this meaningful language can take a variety of physical forms (e.g., can be written in a particular language and printed in a particular book or spoken by a particular person at a particular time), it is only one poem that is actually and potentially manifested in this multiplicity of physical ways. And this one poem cannot consist in physical ingredients (e.g., for written poems, ink or graphite, and for spoken poems, spoken sounds) because only a particular *instance* of a poem can be physically realized in these ways. The sources for a poem's linguistic, conceptual, and sensory ideas include our knowledge of language, our imagination, and our experience. These sources are distinctively *human* sources, since they are each characterized by a particular kind of human consciousness of something. That is why courses in the humanities (e.g., languages, literature, the arts, and history) can provide appropriate materials for the production of artworks of the nonphysical kind.

We can also look to the humanities for knowledge about the *forms* of artifacts. Philosophy can help us think most generally and abstractly about such forms. We have already engaged in some of that sort of philosophical reflection in this chapter. For instance, we have distinguished between artifacts that are works of fine art (meant primarily to be enjoyed) and artifacts that are products of craftsmanship (intended mostly to be used). For more specific and concrete types of the former, we can turn to the specific arts. Courses in literature can introduce us to different literary genres or styles (e.g., poetry, drama, and prose) and even more specific instances of these (e.g., in the case of drama, tragedy, and comedy). Courses in the visual arts cover a range of artwork types (e.g., ceramics, drawing, painting, sculpture, printmaking, photography, film—notice the close tie between form and material in at least some of these cases). When it comes to the more practical and useful artworks, we can learn about different forms by studying such preprofessional subjects as architecture and engineering.

And once we focus our attention on these more utilitarian artworks, it becomes clear that their form tends to be determined by their function to a much higher degree than is the case in the fine arts. For instance, it is no accident that desks (items of furniture that are intended to serve primarily as a workspace of a certain kind) tend to be constructed in such a way as to have a flat horizontal surface of at least a certain minimal size; small, bumpy, and vertically situated objects would be very difficult to use for writing, reading, and other activities for which we typically employ desks. Since this form-function fit is so important in the case of the useful arts, artists, craftspeople, and engineers will need to pay careful attention to both the purposes for which humans use things and the means by which those purposes can be achieved most efficiently and effectively. That is, it will be in their interest to think about both means and ends. To the extent that the means are physical, the natural sciences will be relevant. And since achievement of the ends or goals is intended to facilitate the satisfaction of human desires, and ultimately human well-being or flourishing, the social sciences will be helpful. For instance, the automobile is a useful artifact that enables people to travel great distances over land. In order for our use of these vehicles for this purpose to serve human desires and interests in the best possible way, those who design and manufacture them will need to think about such things as health, safety, comfort, economy, and even prestige. And in order to think about these sorts of things well, they will need to have knowledge not only of physics and biology but also of human psychology, sociology, and economics.

Finally, just as scientific knowledge of these kinds can contribute to productive wisdom, which can lead to beautiful and useful artworks and artifacts, so also at least some useful artifacts (e.g., microscopes and telescopes) can be employed by scientists to further the work of science and thus to yield more theoretical wisdom about the natural and social worlds. So theoretical wisdom and productive wisdom can be mutually beneficial.

Moreover, practical moral wisdom can serve as a guide in the acquisition and application of both scientifically based theoretical wisdom and artistically based productive wisdom. As we saw in the previous chapter, productively wise people can make things that supplement our theoretical wisdom to facilitate our understanding of and response to moral, social, and political problems. But productive knowledge can also be added to theoretical knowledge to make things that serve immoral, harmful, and unjust ends as well. The production of bombs by terrorists is an obvious case in point. A subtler example of the inappropriate use of productive knowledge is the employment of good graphic design skills to market a product that perpetuates harmful or evil practices. In light of the potential to use theoretical and productive knowledge for good or for ill, it is important to remember that both an insightful mind and expert hands require supervision by a discerning heart in order to love and serve people well to the glory of God. In addition, both academic and spiritual disciplines can contribute to the ongoing formation of such minds, hearts, and hands.

A Note on Sources

See Mortimer J. Adler, *Aristotle for Everybody: Difficult Thought Made Easy* (New York: Macmillan, 1978), 61–62, for a more extensive discussion of the distinction between the productive and cooperative practical arts. Plato develops his theory of the forms primarily in his *Republic*. Aristotle discusses his four causes in *Physics*, book 2, chapter 3, and *Metaphysics*, book 5, chapter 2. For more on "tacit" knowledge, see Michael Polanyi's *Personal Knowledge: Towards a Post-Critical Philosophy* (Chicago: University of Chicago Press, 1974). Nicholas Wolterstorff, in his *Art Rethought: The Social Practices of Art* (Oxford: Oxford University Press, 2015), discusses the idea of the arts as social practices and the idea of works of the arts as having different meanings in different practices.

Questions for Reflection and Discussion

1. Do you agree that an artwork is "anything people deliberately make for a purpose" and that artworks include both things made for the purpose of enjoyment and things made to be used?

2. What artwork or artifact other than Michelangelo's *David* can you explain by appealing to Aristotle's four causes? What answers to Aristotle's four questions would you give about this artwork or artifact?

3. In what specific ways can a Christian general education help students become productively wise about the materials, forms, procedures, and purposes involved in artworks?

CHAPTER TWELVE

ACADEMIC DISCIPLINES AND SPIRITUAL DISCIPLINES

LET US RETURN NOW TO OUR DISCUSSION OF THE RELATIONSHIP between Jerusalem and Athens. Citizens of Athens value a general education. Citizens of Jerusalem value a life of Christian devotion.

A general education requires mastery of a set of academic disciplines. Christian devotion requires being mastered by the Holy Spirit through the practice of spiritual disciplines. Can Christian general learners engage in both of these practices at the same time in such a way as to benefit from the interaction between them? The example of Christian philosopher St. Augustine provides a solid basis for an affirmative answer to this question. Augustine's *Confessions* consists in a blend of serious intellectual inquiry and heartfelt personal prayer that can serve as a model for the Christian general education student who seeks to combine the academic and spiritual disciplines in the process of learning for wisdom. From the very first to the very last line of this classic work, Augustine addresses himself to God. The entire work, in which Augustine not only tells the story of his conversion to Christ but also engages in profound and extensive theological and philosophical reflection, takes the form of a prayer to his Lord. And his prolonged prayer both employs a wide range of biblical passages (especially from the Psalms) and takes on a number of forms, including adoration, petition, and confession. Clearly Augustine believed that the study of academic disciplines can be regularly, deliberately, and explicitly combined with the practice of the spiritual discipline of prayer.

Moreover, recall from Chapter Six ("Wisdom in the Biblical Tradition") that Jesus wants us to be wise and that he is the source and embodiment of wisdom. Given these important truths, students at Christian colleges and universities should strive to rely on Jesus for guidance in their disciplined quest for wisdom. Indeed, Augustine develops a view of Jesus as our inner teacher; all the propositional learning we experience is due to Jesus's illuminating our minds to see that some proposition we are thinking about is true. This theory of learning conforms to Jesus's instruction to his disciples not to be called "teacher," since they "have only one teacher, the Messiah" (Matt. 23:10 NLT). Augustine's theory also fits with the prologue of John, which identifies Jesus as the Word of God, who is "the true light which enlightens everyone" (1:9 NRSV). A common human experience suggests Augustine may be right about how we acquire at least some knowledge; everyone knows the difference between being told by a human teacher that something is true and having an interior psychological experience of coming to see that it is true. When this experience is a "flash of insight," it can seem that our minds are illumined so as to enable us to know something about which we were hitherto ignorant. Augustine thinks that Jesus is the only true teacher and giver of knowledge and that he provides this illumination or enlightenment. Whether one accepts this Augustinian thesis or not, one can agree that Jesus continues to be a wise teacher to whom his disciples should turn for instruction and wisdom. So Augustine models for us the study of the academic disciplines facilitated by the spiritual discipline of prayer that includes petitioning Jesus to be our teacher. But what is a discipline? And what are the similarities and differences between academic and spiritual disciplines?

Disciplines as Means to Academic and Spiritual Ends

The dictionary says the noun "discipline" concerns either a means (instruction, training) or an end (knowledge, skill). When considered as a *means*, the word "discipline" implies a process involving effort and control. Sometimes, the source of this control is *external* to the learner or apprentice, and sometimes it is *internal* (and sometimes it is a combination of the two). When the origin of control is external, the teacher or master seeks to motivate the student or disciple by means of rewards ("carrots" to be "eaten") and/or punishments ("sticks" with which to be "beaten"). The cause of control is internal to the extent that it is appropriate to say that learners are exercising *self*-control, and insofar as that is the case, they administer their own rewards and punishments to themselves.

These positive outcomes to be desired and negative consequences to be feared can be either *extrinsic* or *intrinsic* relative to the learning the pupil or trainee is experiencing. A reward or punishment is *extrinsic* to a learning activity when it is not an essential aspect of that activity. High academic grades or marks are an example of a type of extrinsic reward, and fines and demerits or low academic grades are an illustration of extrinsic punishments. The assignment of an "A" grade to a student on an essay that student has written is a standard means by which a teacher can reward the student for excellent academic work—regardless of the specific type of learning the essay reflects. And a required set of fifteen push-ups for inadequate performance in a military training exercise is a characteristic punishment in that sort of context—but again, this penalty is consistent with a wide range of infractions of various kinds. On the other hand, a reward is *intrinsic* to a learning activity when it involves the satisfaction one experiences from acquiring the knowledge or learning the behavior that is the learner's aim. Similarly, a punishment is intrinsic to a learning activity when it takes the form of disappointment about failing to meet an intellectual or behavioral objective. Consequently, it is intrinsically rewarding to be able to recite a poem from memory that one has been trying to learn by heart, and it is an intrinsic punishment not to be able to hit a golf ball without slicing or hooking it.

In sum, when a person is engaged in a discipline in order to learn something, the person's efforts to be successful in that endeavor are under the control of the teacher, the student, or both. And the teacher and/or the student are exercising this control for the sake of the student gaining some extrinsic or intrinsic reward or avoiding some extrinsic or intrinsic punishment. It follows that there are at least four control-source and control-goal combinations: (1) the teacher controls the student by means of the promise (or threat) of extrinsic rewards (or punishments), (2) the teacher controls the student by means of the promise (or threat) of intrinsic rewards (or punishments), (3) the student controls the student by means of the promise (or threat) of extrinsic rewards (or punishments), and (4) the student controls the student by means of the promise (or threat) of intrinsic rewards (or punishments).

It is clear that combination 4 is the ideal toward which any disciplinary practice ought to aspire. In this case, the student has acquired the virtue of self-control with respect to the learning in question, and the student is rewarded merely by the successful attainment of the desired learning goal. As a result, the student is in a position to become her own teacher in this area, and the student is also motivated to achieve her selected learning goals for their own sake rather than for the sake of something else. Students who can discipline themselves do not need to rely on teachers for this purpose, and students whose primary goal is successful learning rather than *recognition* for successful learning (or some other kind of extrinsic reward, such as money or power) are more likely to love learning for its own sake. Finally, such autonomous learners who are motivated by the love of learning will not only be likely to be more successful in their own learning (and more able to extend their learning efforts to other domains), but they will also be prime candidates for becoming effective teachers and masters themselves. That is, they can be disciples who have become capable of making disciples.

We have been discussing the concept of a discipline as a means to the end of learning. Notice that this discussion has treated the concept *generally*. What we have said so far applies to all specific types of disciplines considered as different types of means to different educational goals. In particular, it applies to both academic and spiritual disciplines. Both general education and Christian growth require learning of a disciplined sort for the achievement of the learning goals in these areas. So the practice of academic disciplines and the practice of spiritual disciplines are similar in certain respects. What we said above about a discipline as a means to the end of learning applies to both of them. They differ in their specific learning *goals*. The main specific proximate goal of Christian general learning is, as we discussed in Chapter Three, *intellectual formation*—that is, the emergence and shaping of a Christian mind. The main specific proximate goal of Christian growth is *spiritual formation*—that is, the maturation and eventual perfection of the whole Christian person into the likeness of Jesus Christ.

There are at least two ways in which the disciplined learning that aims at intellectual formation differs from the disciplined learning that is directed toward spiritual formation. The former is a *natural* process that results primarily in *cognitive and intellectual* change. The latter is primarily a *supernatural* process that results principally in *moral and spiritual* change. So these two types of discipline differ in both the means they involve and the specific end to which they are directed. To say that Christian general learners employ *natural* means to achieve the intellectual formation for which they strive is to say that their efforts are both necessary and sufficient to produce this result. And the result in question is primarily intellectual—it involves the acquisition of propositional, recognitional, and procedural knowledge characteristic of the academic disciplines (considered as an area of study comprising both means and ends). To say that Christians engaged in spiritual disciplines employ *supernatural* means to facilitate spiritual formation is to say that, though their own human efforts are a necessary part of the process, their work alone is not sufficient to produce this result. What is needed in addition for genuine spiritual growth and development is God's wise, gracious, and powerful work through the Holy Spirit in the disciple's mind and heart. Though followers of Jesus Christ must engage in spiritual disciplines in order to put themselves in a position to allow God to work in their lives most effectively, it is God who transforms them supernaturally into the likeness of Christ. And though this process of spiritual transformation includes growth in knowledge (including, most importantly, growth in experiential knowledge of God), the end result is more inclusive: participation in the very life of God.

Christian general learners can practice the academic and spiritual disciplines not only in such a way as to allow these disciplines to enable these students to experience simultaneous intellectual, moral, and spiritual growth but also in such a way that these disciplines will work together for increased effectiveness. For instance, the more we come to know about God directly through academic theological reflection and indirectly through the scientific study of the world God created (including the world of human beings created in God's image), the more intellectual resources we will have—resources that can facilitate the spiritual disciplines of worshiping God, stewarding God's creation, and loving and serving our fellow divine image-bearers. And the more we engage in our academic studies humbly, worshipfully, and prayerfully, with openness to the role of Jesus Christ as our teacher and the Holy Spirit as our guide, the more we will be motivated to learn about God and the world God made and to use our knowledge to serve and obey God.

It is also important to point out that students can and should engage in academic and spiritual disciplines both individually and communally. For both academic and spiritual purposes, it is important for Christian students to practice the disciplines of solitude, silence, and study. These disciplines of withdrawal and resignation put individual students in a position to be transformed by what they learn from the study of their textbooks and the Scriptures without the interference of cultural influences that tend to prevent them from fully understanding, appreciating, and accepting what is true, good, beautiful, and pleasing to God. But it is also important for academic and spiritual purposes that Christian students practice the disciplines of fellowship, conversation, and debate. These disciplines of engagement and interaction put students in a position to practice loving and serving each other and to learn from each other by humbly subjecting themselves to each other's guidance and correction.

A Disciplined Approach to Worldview Construction

So far in this chapter, we have discussed the nature of a "discipline" as a process of instruction or training, and we have compared and contrasted the academic and spiritual disciplines for the purpose of thinking about how students can exercise them together. In this section, we will think about how students can engage in both academic and spiritual disciplines to use the kind of knowledge definitive of the standard academic disciplines to answer four important worldview questions discussed by Dallas Willard. These are (1) the reality question ("What is real?"), (2) the question of well-being or blessedness ("Who has it made?"), (3) the character question ("Who is a really good person?"), and (4) the development question ("How does one become a genuinely good person?"). Every worldview, including the Christian worldview, provides answers to these questions. Indeed, worldviews can be defined and distinguished in terms of their differing answers to these questions. Though the three worldview questions introduced in Chapter Nine ("Learning for Theoretical Wisdom") are somewhat different from Willard's four worldview questions, they overlap to a large extent. The first two questions in Chapter Nine ("What is the world like?" and "Why does a world exist?") provide more specific ways of answering Willard's question 1: "What is real?" And the third question in Chapter Nine ("What is the place of human beings in the world?") is a general way of inquiring about what Willard's questions 2, 3, and 4 concern.

Clearly, students will need to exercise and draw on the academic disciplines to arrive at answers to these four questions. To answer question 1, they will need to make use of philosophy, natural theology, revealed theology, mathematics, logic, the natural sciences, and the social sciences. That is, they will need to employ all of the theoretical academic disciplines. But the most important disciplines among those on this list are natural and revealed theology. That's because the most important question about reality we can ask is whether there is a perfect personal God who created the universe and then created us in God's image for God's loving purposes. Knowing the answer to that question is crucial for determining the answers to the remaining worldview questions. If there is a God who created us for his loving purposes, then there is good reason to think that our prospects for well-being and genuine goodness will involve our knowledge of and response to God's will for us. If such a God does not exist, then the remaining three questions will have a different answer or no answer at all.

If the answer to question 1 is that a loving creator God exists, then we will need to employ theology and the sciences, but especially psychology, history, and the social sciences, to answer questions 2, 3, and 4 (though insofar as our well-being in general depends on our *physical* well-being, the sciences of physics, chemistry, and biology will be helpful as well). The more we understand God's purposes and will for us through our study of theology, the more we will know what would be best for us and what would make us good. The more we understand psychology, the more we will understand how we can thrive personally and excel morally given the nature that God has given us. And the more we understand history and the social sciences, the more we will see how we can order our collective lives in such a way as to form communities characterized by the sorts of relationships God created us to cultivate and enjoy.

But though the academic disciplines will be important for these purposes, they will not be enough. In order to answer all four worldview questions as completely and adequately as possible, we will need to practice spiritual disciplines as well. Our exercise of spiritual disciplines for the purpose of answering these questions will provide us with an *experimental* means of acquiring knowledge about them. Practicing the presence of God and communing with God in prayer and worship will be a crucial means of confirming the reality of God. Relying on God's promises as we live our lives in the midst of difficult and uncertain circumstances will be an important way to have a rich and fulfilling experience of God's sustaining love on an ongoing basis. Attending to the teaching and example of Jesus and his most devoted followers throughout history will enable us to confirm what kind of person is genuinely good. And regularly obeying God's commandments and putting Jesus's teaching into practice will help us learn how we can become the kind of people we have learned to admire and who consistently please God through their loving, faithful, and self-sacrificial service.

Genuine wisdom requires knowing the answers to these worldview questions. The best learning for this kind of wisdom requires involvement with both the academic and spiritual disciplines. Students who combine these disciplines effectively are putting themselves in a position to acquire a Christian mind and a godly character. And as they continue to grow in theoretical, practical, and productive wisdom through their academic and spiritual discipline, they will become more and more capable of living a good and blessed life both individually and communally. In doing so, they will show that they can be citizens of both Jerusalem and Athens.

Learning as Worship and Worship as Learning

In Chapter One, we reflected on learning. We will close this chapter—and this book—by thinking about the relationship between learning and worship. Recall that learning is a natural process that results in a gain of knowledge of some kind or other (e.g., propositional, recognitional, or procedural). This book has focused on the kind of learning that should characterize a Christian general education: learning for wisdom (theoretical, practical, and productive). Now we will explore what it means to engage in this sort of learning as a means of worship and even as a *form* of worship. After that we will investigate ways in which the activity of worship can be a means or form of learning.

But what is worship? Worship is an orientation toward a person or thing that involves an attitude of reverence, adoration, or devotion toward that person or thing. An attitude of this sort is based on or consists in esteem for the object of worship as sufficiently important to be *worthy* of our reverence, adoration, or devotion. We can use Augustine's language to characterize worship as an attitude of *love for someone or something we regard or treat as worthy of our highest esteem*. And we can tell what a person worships by observing how that person behaves. People behave *sacrificially* toward the people or things they worship. They are willing to sacrifice valuable resources such as time, attention, energy, honor, health, and sometimes even life itself for that which they worship. In short, insofar as people worship someone or something, they love that person or thing to such an extent that there is nothing they love more.

From a Christian standpoint, only the Triune God is worthy of worship. And yet many people worship persons or things other than God. In that case, though they treat and perhaps regard those persons or things as worthy of worship, they really are not. Everything other than God is lower than God on the Great Chain of Being and so is inferior in value to God. The worship of any of these lesser things is *idolatry*. Idolatry involves putting anything other than God in the place of God. Obvious forms of idolatry today are the worship of money, power, and prestige. Less obvious forms of idolatry include the worship of knowledge, health, and even service. Though these objects of affection and desire are good things and are better than the former three (which are also good things), they are still not suitable to serve as a focal point of our ultimate concern. Only God the Father, Son, and Holy Spirit is.

Christian general learners should strive to avoid idolatry and to worship only God by means of their Christian general education. It is easy to treat learning as a tool for self-advancement or even self-glorification rather than as a vehicle for furthering God's purposes and glorifying God. Even the familiar advice, characteristic of the general education tradition, to love learning for its own sake can lead to a subtle form of idolatry. Though nobler than the love of money, the love of learning is still inferior to the love of God.

But it is possible to learn to engage in Christian general learning as a means of worshiping God. Though such worship should not and cannot take the place of a worship *service*, it can nonetheless be an appropriate and valuable extension of the special sort of worship in which Christians participate in church on Sunday. What can make it a suitable and worthwhile form of worship is that it involves praising God for what God gives and who God is in addition to offering God's gifts back to him for the sake of Christian service.

As students engage in Christian general learning for wisdom, they can learn to welcome the truth, goodness, and beauty they discover, experience, and enjoy as gifts from God, who is the source of these things. In order to be in the best position to do this, students can start their studies with prayer, as Augustine did. James urges any of his readers who lack wisdom to "ask God, who gives generously to all without finding fault, and it will be given to [them]" (James 1:5 NIV). He also says that "every good and perfect gift is from above, coming down from the Father of the heavenly lights" (1:17 NIV). With these truths in mind, Christian students can learn to be grateful to God as the source of truth, goodness, and beauty and as the giver of the theoretical, practical, and productive wisdom we acquire as we use our God-given minds and hearts and as God assists us with our study and learning. And their gratitude can be turned to praise and worship as they delight in both the gifts and the Giver.

Moreover, Christian students can learn to worship God in their learning by offering back to God the wisdom God has enabled them to have. After all, God blesses us in order to serve him by being a blessing to others. This is surely what James had in mind when he addressed the wise among his readers: "Who is wise and understanding among you? Let them show it by their good life, by deeds done in the humility that comes from wisdom" (3:13 NIV). When we offer our God-given wisdom back to God for the sake of God's Kingdom, we are worshiping God by exalting him as the worthy recipient of our best gifts. And what better gifts could we give to God than our love and wisdom? When we do so, we are pledging to use the fruits of our learning—our reason, knowledge, and wisdom—ministerially rather than magisterially. That is, we are using them for God's purposes rather than for our own selfish and even idolatrous purposes. So Christian students can learn to worship God through their learning both by praising God for his gift of wisdom and by offering this gift back to God in the service of his Kingdom.

But Christian students can also learn through worshiping God. That is, simply by engaging in worship, Christians can acquire knowledge. Central to the type of knowledge Christians can gain in worship is *knowing how to love, serve, and glorify God and knowing how to love, serve, and cherish the people of God.* Whereas the kind of learning we had in mind in the first part of this section is primarily the conscious process of *being informed*, the kind of learning that is more central at this point is the relatively unconscious (or subconscious) process of *being formed.* And whereas the process of being informed is mostly a *mental and intellectual* process involving the *mind*, the process of being formed is mostly a *moral and spiritual* process involving the *heart.* When we are informed, our minds are improved by superior thinking. And when we are formed, our hearts are enhanced by superior desiring. Both kinds of betterment are essential for Christian growth. We need to know and to love what God knows and loves (as much as God makes it possible for us to do so), and we need to know and to love God.

In sum, Christian students need to learn, and they need to worship. And they should aspire to worship as they learn and to learn as they worship. Learning and worshiping can be mutually reinforcing activities. But in order for this ongoing cycle of reinforcement to be most effective, the sort of learning that leads to worship should take place primarily in the classroom, the laboratory, and the studio; and the sort of worship that leads to learning should happen mostly in the chapel and the church sanctuary. Particular types of practices are most effectively implemented in particular types of contexts. Academic practices (teaching, learning, lecturing, and discussing) are most effective in academic contexts, and ecclesial practices (preaching, confessing, singing, and chanting) are most effective in ecclesial contexts. Even so, though Christian general learners should regularly visit both the classroom and the church (and chapel), they should also seek to learn and to worship at all times and in all places. When they do so, they will show themselves to be citizens of both Jerusalem and Athens.

A Note on Sources

See Augustine, *Confessions*, 2nd ed. (Indianapolis: Hackett, 2006), translated by F. J. Sheed, edited by Michael P. Foley, and introduced by Peter Brown, for an excellent edition of this great work. Augustine develops his view of Jesus as our inner teacher in his dialogue *De Magistro* (*On the Teacher*). Dallas Willard discusses his four worldview questions in *Knowing Christ Today: Why We Can Trust Spiritual Knowledge* (New York: HarperOne, 2009), 45–50. In *On the Free Choice of the Will*, Augustine defines God as "that to which nothing is superior," a conception that makes God superior to us (and everything else) in value, and so worthy of worship. In *Desiring the Kingdom* (Grand Rapids: Baker Academic, 2009), chapter 6, James K. A. Smith talks about the role of worship in Christian higher education.

Questions for Reflection and Discussion

1. To what extent are your learning disciplines characterized by self-control, motivated by a desire for intrinsic rewards, aimed at both

academic and spiritual ends, and exercised both individually and communally? Explain.

2. What are Willard's four worldview questions, and how does answering them adequately require the exercise of both academic and spiritual disciplines?

3. How can Christian general education students worship while learning and learn while worshiping? How can learning and worship work together to both inform and form Christian general learners for maximal academic and spiritual growth?

ACKNOWLEDGEMENTS

I STARTED WRITING THIS BOOK ON A WESTMONT COLLEGE SABBATical in the fall of 1998. Shortly after that, I got busy on a different book project, and didn't return in earnest to this one until another sabbatical in the spring of 2012. The lengthy gap between the initial conception and final publication of *Learning for Wisdom* was a blessing. I learned a lot about learning, wisdom, and learning for wisdom during that period of time, and the book is better than it would have been if I had finished it earlier.

I am grateful to three Westmont provosts: Stan Gaede, who originally encouraged me to write this book (and who read the entire manuscript many years later), Shirley Mullen, who supported me along the way, and Mark Sargent, who suggested I ask Abilene Christian University Press to publish it.

I am also indebted to the Westmont faculty and staff who participated in the Summer 2002 Liberal Arts Workshop led by Chris Hoeckley. It was during this workshop that I wrote an essay on the liberal arts that eventually became Chapter Two of this volume ("General Learning"). I was pleased that Jeffry Davis, whom I met years later at a Gaede Institute for the Liberal Arts Conversation, found this essay online and shared it with an appreciative faculty at Wheaton College.

Various scholars read portions of the book and gave me helpful feedback. These people include Tremper Longman, who read a draft of Chapter Six ("Wisdom in the Biblical Tradition"), Gregg Ten Elshof and Amos Yong, who read a draft of Chapter Seven ("Wisdom in the Asian Tradition"), David Vander Laan, who read and commented on selected chapters of the book, and Ken Boa, who suggested a new way of organizing some of the book's material.

Conversations about the books' topics with friends and colleagues over the years helped me shape my ideas. David Ross and Charles Hall brainstormed with me in the early stages during my fall 1998 sabbatical. Greg Spencer and I have had recurring discussions about the oratorical and philosophical approaches to the liberal arts. A talk with Telford Work at a crucial juncture facilitated a decision about the scope of the work. And Jason Fikes helped me frame the project in such a way as to reach a wider audience.

A former student of mine, Melissa Christensen, read an earlier version of the entire manuscript and evaluated it from a student's point of view. I am thankful for her careful reading and suggested revisions.

The Westmont Professional Development Committee provided me with three summer grants to support my work on this book over the years. Finally, I am grateful for my wife Jennifer's love, encouragement, support, and wisdom throughout the years I worked on this book.

INDEX

Tables are indicated by *t* after the page number.

CPSIA information can be obtained
at www.ICGtesting.com
Printed in the USA
LVOW03s2242290317
528986LV00006B/6/P

9 781684 260102